CINEMATIC CLASSICS

This book belongs to

Acknowledgments
Special thanks to Lucasfilm Ltd for their invaluable assistance
and for providing the artwork for this book.

First published in the UK in 2025 by Studio Press Books, an imprint of Bonnier Books UK,
5th Floor, HYLO, 105 Bunhill Row, London, EC1Y 8LZ
bonnierbooks.co.uk

Copyright © and TM 2025 LUCASFILM LTD.
All rights reserved. No part of this publication may be reproduced or transmitted in any form or by any means, electronic, or mechanical, including photocopying, recording, or by any information storage and retrieval system, without permission in writing from the publisher.

1 3 5 7 9 10 8 6 4 2

ISBN 978-1-83587-149-2

Text adapted by Tom Huddleston
Edited by Georgina Kyriacou
Designed by Maddox Philpot
Cover illustrated by Alexander Ward
Production by Nick Read

The authorised representative in the EEA is Bonnier Books UK (Ireland) Limited.
Registered office address: Floor 3, Block 3, Miesian Plaza
50–58 Baggot Street Lower, Dublin 2, D02 Y754, Ireland.
compliance@bonnierbooks.ie

A CIP catalogue record for this book is available from the British Library

Printed and bound in China

By 1980, as I was about to turn 15, it was finally time to see The Empire Strikes Back, and I so remember that day, running through the mall with my friends, going to newsstands and bookstores and seeing all of the book covers for the film that had just opened in theaters. From the Gone with the Wind inspired poster that was the book cover, to the Marvel comics adaptation, the beautiful art was everywhere, and there was nothing in the world that was as cool as that to me.

The Empire Strikes Back was a much darker film, as we began to get to know more about the characters, but with new and exciting characters, from the legendary Boba Fett to the wise Master Jedi, Yoda, who has become as iconic as Darth Vader. We got to see new fantastic worlds, with exciting new creatures, ships and vehicles, and a snow planet, a swamp planet, and a planet with a city in the clouds – it was beyond breathtaking.

It continued to fuel and inspire the creative path of so many other people all over the world. No film had ever had a sequel that delivered as this one did, and to many it will be their favorite. From the grand battle on the ice planet Hoth, this was definitely the Empire striking back, with space battles and epic lightsaber battles that define the *Star Wars* saga. We dive deeper into the Force with Luke doing his Jedi training under Yoda, and we get to know more of the Galactic Empire, and we see Darth Vader's boss, Emperor Palpatine.

Another spectacular out-of-this-world tale, from the mind of George Lucas, and all of it realized and visualized by artists and designers of all kinds, defining and setting the bar on what was second to none in masterful creativity and storytelling.

The artwork that first brought this second installment to life fill the pages of this new retelling. It continues to illustrate the creativity and imagination that went into this sequel film, and again inspired audiences and is here to inspire you.

Troy Alders
Art Director, Lucasfilm

CINEMATIC CLASSICS

THE EMPIRE STRIKES BACK

It is a dark time for the Rebellion. Although the Death Star has been destroyed, Imperial troops have driven the Rebel forces from their hidden base and pursued them across the galaxy.

Evading the dreaded Imperial Starfleet, a group of freedom fighters led by Luke Skywalker has established a new secret base on the remote ice world of Hoth.

The evil lord Darth Vader, obsessed with finding young Skywalker, has dispatched thousands of remote probes into the far reaches of space....

Far out in the depths of space, the Imperial Star Destroyer drifted silently. Its vast underside released a number of small, unmanned projectiles. The probes fired their engines, blasting out across the galaxy in search of the Rebels' newest hideout. It wasn't long before one of them found its target.

EPISODE V: THE EMPIRE STRIKES BACK

Rocketing through the atmosphere of Hoth, the probe crashed into the planet's snowy surface. From the impact crater a gleaming black droid emerged, its sensors whirring.

A short distance away, the rebel hero Luke Skywalker peered through his macrobinoculars. Seated astride a two-legged creature known as a tauntaun, he used the comlink on his wrist to radio his friend Han Solo. They'd been sent out to patrol the area around the Rebels' secret base. 'There isn't enough life on this ice cube to fill a space cruiser,' Han grumbled. 'Sensors are placed. I'm going back.'

Concept art for an Imperial probe droid. **Ralph McQuarrie**.

CINEMATIC CLASSICS

Luke promised to follow, just as soon as he checked out the meteorite whose smoke trail he'd observed moments before. But before he could reach it, his tauntaun began to gabble fearfully.

There was a sudden deafening roar! Before Luke could react, a huge, white-furred paw swiped at him, knocking him unconscious. It belonged to an ice-beast called a wampa, which stood three metres tall and had huge teeth and claws. It dispatched Luke's tauntaun with a single blow. Then it began dragging Luke away through the snow.

Back at the Rebel headquarters, codenamed Echo Base, Han Solo returned from his patrol. Entering through a hangar teeming with Rebel troops, he made his way to the command centre to be greeted by the officer in charge, General Rieekan.

Concept art for a Rebel trooper riding a tauntaun.
RALPH MCQUARRIE

'General, I gotta leave,' Han stated. He still owed a lot of money to the infamous gangster Jabba the Hutt and knew that he'd never be safe until the debt was paid.

Rieekan nodded regretfully. 'A death mark's not an easy thing to live with,' he said. 'You're a good fighter, Solo. I hate to lose you.'

EPISODE V: THE EMPIRE STRIKES BACK

Concept art for a Rebel trooper outside of Echo Base. **Ralph McQuarrie**

From across the command centre, a young woman glanced in Han's direction. It was Princess Leia Organa, whose brave actions had helped destroy the Death Star. She followed Han into an adjoining corridor and called out his name. 'I thought you had decided to stay,' she said.

Han shook his head. A run-in with one of Jabba's henchmen on the planet Ord Mantell had reminded him how much danger he was in.

'We need you,' Leia continued.

Han turned. '*We* need?' he asked. 'What about, *you* need?'

CINEMATIC CLASSICS

'I need?' Leia shot back. 'I don't know what you're talking about.'

'Come on!' Han cajoled. 'You want me to stay because of the way you feel about me.'

Leia stared at him in disbelief. 'You're imagining things.'

Concept art for the headquarters of Rebel command centre, featuring portable equipment that could be carried in. RALPH MCQUARRIE

EPISODE V: THE EMPIRE STRIKES BACK

'Am I?' Han demanded. 'Then why are you following me? Afraid I was going to leave without giving you a goodbye kiss?'

Leia lost her patience. 'I'd just as soon kiss a Wookiee,' she snapped.

Han stormed back to the hangar where his fur-covered Wookiee co-pilot Chewbacca was working to fix their battered old spaceship, the *Millennium Falcon*. But it wasn't long before they were interrupted by two droids: gleaming protocol unit C-3PO and his diminutive counterpart, the astromech R2-D2. They'd been sent to ask Han if he knew the whereabouts of Luke Skywalker.

Suddenly concerned, Han consulted the deck officer only to discover that Luke still hadn't returned from patrol. 'Then we'll have to go out on tauntauns,' he said without hesitation.

An officer looked at him in horror. 'Sir, the temperature's dropping too rapidly!'

'That's right,' Han said, leaping onto the nearest mount. 'And my friend's out in it.'

CINEMATIC CLASSICS

Concept art for the wampa. JOE JOHNSTON

EPISODE V: THE EMPIRE STRIKES BACK

Before anyone could stop him, Han rode out into the frozen wasteland.

In a hidden ice cave, Luke Skywalker regained consciousness only to find himself hanging upside down by his ankles. A short distance away, the wampa was feasting on the bloody remains of Luke's tauntaun. Luke knew it was only a matter of time before the beast turned its attention to him.

Looking around, he spotted his lightsaber, an energy-bladed weapon used by the Jedi. It was just out of reach. Closing his eyes, Luke summoned the power of the mystical energy field known as the Force. The saber's hilt began to tremble.

The wampa rose to its feet, lumbering towards Luke. Just in time, the saber leapt into Luke's hand. He ignited the blue blade, cutting himself free. Then he slashed at the wampa, severing the beast's arm. The wampa howled in rage and pain as Luke fled, out into the raging snowstorm.

Concept art storyboard showing Luke Skywalker attempting to master the Force. RALPH MCQUARRIE

CINEMATIC CLASSICS

At Echo Base, Princess Leia received the news she had been dreading. No one had heard from either Han or Luke, and with temperatures plummeting, they had no choice but to close the shield doors. Chewbacca howled with despair as the heavy durasteel barrier slid shut. Threepio hurried away, muttering worriedly.

Concept art storyboard for Luke Skywalker's semi-conscious hallucination of Obi-Wan Kenobi.
JOE JOHNSTON

Out on the ice plains, Luke Skywalker lay helpless in the snow. Suddenly, a shimmering vision appeared before him. It was Obi-Wan Kenobi, the Jedi Master who had taught Luke the ways of the Force, only to die at the hands of Darth Vader.

'You will go to the Dagobah system,' Obi-Wan said. 'There you will learn from Yoda, the Jedi Master who instructed me.'

EPISODE V: THE EMPIRE STRIKES BACK

Luke reached out, but the vision faded. It was replaced by the silhouette of a tauntaun, and a figure leaping down from the creature's back.

Han Solo ran to Luke's side, finding his friend already unconscious. He was about to return to his tauntaun when the beast keeled over, unable to withstand the sub-zero temperatures. Han knew what he had to do.

He dragged Luke back to the tauntaun. With trembling hands, he unclipped Luke's lightsaber from his belt. Igniting the laser sword, Han sliced at the tauntaun's belly, allowing its innards to spill out.

Concept art for the head of a tauntaun.
RALPH MCQUARRIE

'This may smell bad, kid,' Han said apologetically as he placed Luke inside the tauntaun's steaming belly, 'but it'll keep you warm, until I can get the shelter up.'

Early the next morning, a snowspeeder patrol was dispatched to search for the missing Rebels. A pilot named Zev Senesca picked up a transmission from Han Solo. He spotted the hastily erected shelter and swooped in to pick them up.

CINEMATIC CLASSICS

Concept art for Han, Leia and the medical droid waiting for Luke to heal in the Hoth sick bay.
RALPH MCQUARRIE

Luke was rushed to the medical bay and placed inside a bacta tank for rapid healing. Under the care of a 2-1B medical droid, Luke was soon well enough to receive visitors.

C-3PO and R2-D2 expressed their relief that Luke was on the mend. Chewie rumbled warmly, and even Han looked pleased. 'You look strong enough to pull the ears off a gundark.' He grinned.

Then he turned to Leia. 'Well, your Worship. Looks like you managed to keep me around for a little while longer.'

'I had nothing to do with it,' the Princess told him. 'General Rieekan thinks it's dangerous for any ships to leave the system until we've activated the energy field.'

EPISODE V: THE EMPIRE STRIKES BACK

'That's a good story.' Han chuckled. 'I think you just can't bear to let a gorgeous guy like me out of your sight.'

Leia scowled. 'Why, you stuck-up, half-witted, scruffy-looking nerf herder!' To prove Han wrong, she walked over to Luke and planted a kiss on his lips. Han could only watch as she strode away, leaving Luke grinning in his medcenter bed.

In the command centre, General Rieekan received word that a suspicious object had been detected. It was sending out a weak signal, possibly an Imperial code. Han and Chewbacca volunteered to investigate. They soon spotted a mysterious droid floating near the base. Han crept close with his blaster, and on his second shot, the droid self-destructed.

Concept art for the ion cannon "Rebel Big Gun Control Booth." RALPH MCQUARRIE

CINEMATIC CLASSICS

Concept art for Darth Vader pacing on the bridge of an Imperial Star Destroyer. RALPH MCQUARRIE

Now the Rebels knew they were in trouble. The probe droid must have been sent by the Empire. The Imperial fleet wouldn't be too far behind. It was time for the Rebels to leave.

In a distant part of the galaxy, Darth Vader stood on the bridge of his vast Star Dreadnought, the *Executor*, as the ship picked up the probe droid's signal. 'That's it,' Vader told the officer on duty, Captain Piett. 'The Rebels are there.'

A second officer named Admiral Ozzel wasn't so sure, but Vader overruled him. He ordered his military commander, General Veers, to prepare his troops for battle.

EPISODE V: THE EMPIRE STRIKES BACK

Echo Base was a hive of activity as the Rebels prepared to evacuate. Han and Chewie were working on the *Falcon* when Luke came to say goodbye. He received a furry hug from Chewbacca, but he had no idea what to say to Han. Once again the smuggler had saved his life, but he couldn't say when or if they'd see each other again.

In the command centre, Rebel sensors had spotted Imperial ships approaching. Rieekan ordered all power to the shields until they could clear the base. On the *Executor*, Darth Vader was furious that his fleet had been detected so easily. 'Admiral Ozzel came out of lightspeed too close to the system,' he seethed.

Concept art for the original design of Darth Vader's Imperial Star Destroyer. NILO RODIS-JAMERO

CINEMATIC CLASSICS

Activating a screen on the wall, he contacted the Admiral. As Ozzel turned, Vader reached out with the Force. The Admiral began to choke, clutching at his throat. Captain Piett tried not to react as his commanding officer collapsed lifelessly to the floor. 'You are in command now, *Admiral* Piett,' Vader told him.

In the hangar at Echo Base, Princess Leia briefed a group of Rebel fighter pilots. It was their mission to escort the escaping transports safely out

Composite shot of the Rebel ships breaking through the Imperial blockade. **Terry Chostner**

EPISODE V: THE EMPIRE STRIKES BACK

of the system. A weapon called an ion cannon would help to clear any Imperial ships out of their path.

As the first Rebel transport soared away, the ion cannon fired. An advancing Star Destroyer received several blasts, giving the Rebels the space they needed to jump to lightspeed. In the hangar, the pilots cheered.

But on the surface of Hoth, Rebel soldiers had detected something approaching. As they hurried to dig defensive trenches, they heard what sounded like giant footsteps. Soon they saw a line of vast machines: armoured transports on huge, towering legs.

As the Imperial walkers neared Echo Base, a squadron of two-man snowspeeders scrambled to repel the attack. Codenamed Rogue Group, they were led by none other than Luke Skywalker.

The speeders opened fire, but their blaster shots had little effect on the walkers' heavy armour. Luke had an idea. 'Rogue Group, use your harpoons and tow cables,' he ordered. 'Go for the legs. It might be our only chance of stopping them.'

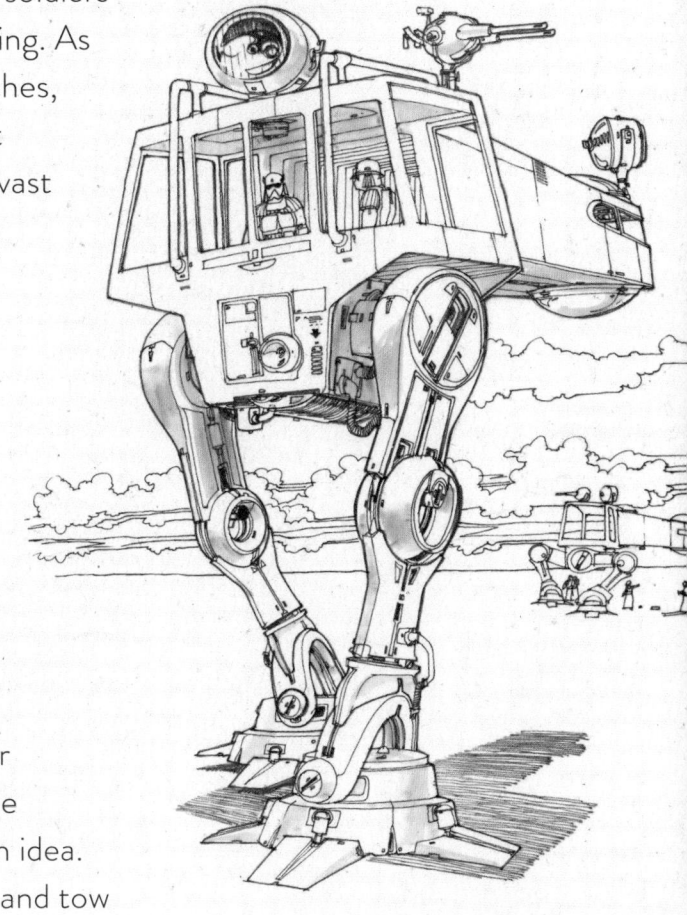

Concept art for a scout walker. **JOE JOHNSTON**

CINEMATIC CLASSICS

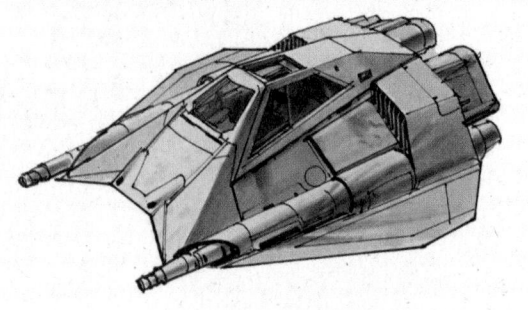

Suddenly, a blast from one of the walkers struck his speeder. Turning, he saw to his horror that his tail gunner Dak had been killed. He could no longer fire his harpoon, but he could offer covering fire as another pilot, Wedge Antilles, started his attack run.

Wedge's tail gunner fired a magnetic harpoon, hitting the leg of one walker. With the attached tow cable, their snowspeeder circled several times, trapping the walker's legs. 'Detach cable,' Wedge called before flying clear of the armoured vehicle. When the walker tried to take a step, the cable tightened and the great machine crashed to the ground, allowing the snowspeeders to swoop in and blast it to pieces.

Concept art for the Rebel's snowspeeders. **RALPH MCQUARRIE**

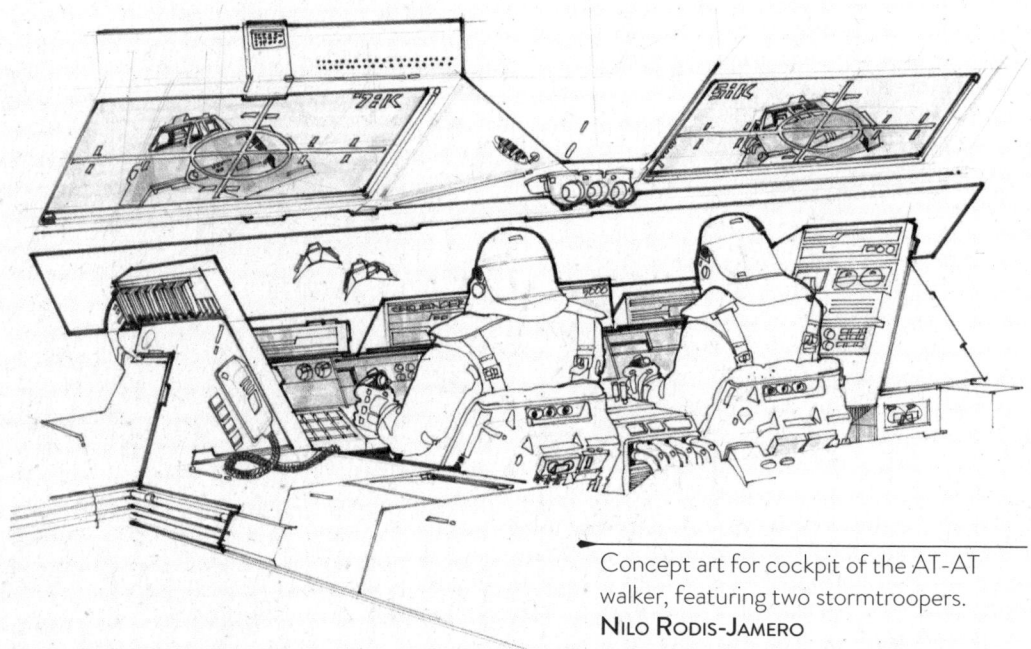

Concept art for cockpit of the AT-AT walker, featuring two stormtroopers. **NILO RODIS-JAMERO**

EPISODE V: THE EMPIRE STRIKES BACK

But Rogue Group's celebrations were short-lived. As the Imperial assault continued, Zev's ship was shot down and Luke took another blast, sending his speeder spiralling to the ground. He barely escaped before a walker's metal foot crashed down, flattening his ship into the snow.

Inside Echo Base, the Rebels hurried to complete the evacuation. One of the few ships remaining was the *Millennium Falcon*, which still needed last-minute repairs. Leaving Chewbacca to fix the ship, Han headed to the command centre, where he found Princess Leia still at her post.

'You've got your clearance to leave,' she told Han curtly.

'Don't worry, I'll leave,' he shot back. 'First I'm going to get you to your ship.'

'Your Highness, we must take this last transport,' Threepio agreed. 'It's our only hope.'

Concept art for the docking bay of the Rebel base on Hoth, featuring Rebel troops running.
RALPH MCQUARRIE

CINEMATIC CLASSICS

On the surface, General Veers targeted the Rebels' shield generator with maximum firepower. As Echo Base took more hits, the ground shook violently and tunnels began to collapse.

Han and Leia ran to catch the last transport, but soon found their way blocked by fallen ice. All Han could do was radio the Rebels and tell them to take off. Leia would join him on the *Falcon*.

As the Imperial walkers approached the base, Luke used a magnetic harpoon to attach himself to the underside of one of the vast machines. Using his lightsaber, he cut open a hatch in the walker's belly and tossed an explosive charge inside. Then he dropped back to the snow. Moments later, the walker's cockpit exploded and it toppled sideways, gushing smoke.

In the main hangar, Han tried desperately to get the *Millennium Falcon* off the ground as a platoon of snowtroopers fired at the ship. 'This bucket of bolts is never going to get us past that blockade!' Leia protested.

'This baby's got a few surprises left in her, sweetheart,' Han assured her, using the ship's guns to repel the troopers.

'Punch it,' he told Chewie, and the *Falcon* roared into life, soaring from the hangar. Darth Vader arrived just in time to see the ship leave. He knew

EPISODE V: THE EMPIRE STRIKES BACK

that capturing the *Millennium Falcon* was his best hope of finding Luke Skywalker.

Out on the plains of Hoth, Luke also saw the *Falcon* depart. He strode to his X-wing fighter, where R2-D2 was waiting for him. As they blasted out of Hoth's atmosphere, Artoo began to beep questioningly. 'There's nothing wrong, Artoo,' Luke reassured the little droid. 'I'm just setting a new course. We're not going to regroup with the others. We're going to the Dagobah system.'

Concept art for Luke crawling out of his snowspeeder after being shot down. **RALPH MCQUARRIE**

CINEMATIC CLASSICS

While Luke's small fighter had no trouble slipping past the Imperial blockade, the *Millennium Falcon* was not so lucky. Under heavy fire from four pursuing TIE fighters, the old freighter was about to be pinned down by a group of enclosing Star Destroyers. A series of evasive manoeuvres forced the Destroyers into a near-collision, but the TIE fighters were still closing in. Han knew it was time to make the jump to lightspeed.

But when he tried to activate the hyperdrive, nothing happened. Threepio informed them that the mechanism had been damaged.

As Han and Chewie struggled to fix the hyperdrive, they felt something strike the ship. Outside the cockpit, they saw a vast expanse of tumbling rocks: an asteroid field.

Concept art for the *Millennium Falcon* flying in space. **RALPH MCQUARRIE**

EPISODE V: THE EMPIRE STRIKES BACK

To Princess Leia's shock, Han told Chewie to take the *Falcon* deeper into the asteroids. 'They'd be crazy to follow us, wouldn't they?' he reasoned as huge boulders spiralled past the ship, slamming into two of the pursuing TIE fighters.

The hail of rocks grew heavier, until even Han started to look worried. 'We're going to get pulverised if we stay out here much longer,' Leia argued, and Han could only agree.

He piloted the *Falcon* towards one of the larger asteroids. They skimmed over the surface and down into a canyon, forcing the last two TIE fighters into an explosive collision. Then Han gestured up ahead. 'There,' he said. 'That looks pretty good.'

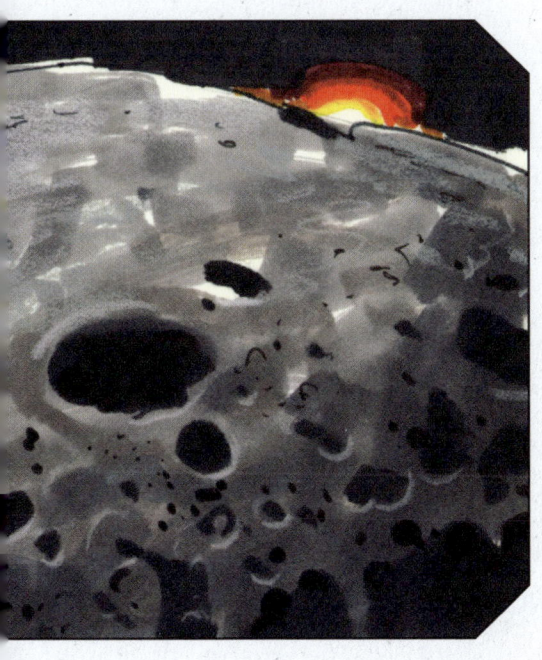

The *Falcon* arced gracefully over the asteroid's surface and then dropped, vanishing into a large, cylindrical cave. 'I hope you know what you're doing,' Leia murmured as they were swallowed by the darkness.

Meanwhile, Luke Skywalker piloted his X-wing towards the surface of Dagobah, descending through a dense curtain of cloud. The sensors had picked up massive life readings, but no signs of civilisation. Luke's ship crashed through a wall of foliage, then splashed down into a pool of dark water.

CINEMATIC CLASSICS

Fog covered the ground and strange animal calls sounded in the gloom as Luke climbed from the cockpit. The X-wing shuddered in the bubbling swamp, sending Artoo toppling into the water.

At first the little droid seemed unharmed, using his periscope to navigate to land. He didn't notice a dark shape breaking the surface behind him. As

Concept art for Luke and his X-wing in a bog on Dagobah, featuring R2-D2. **Ralph McQuarrie**

EPISODE V: THE EMPIRE STRIKES BACK

Luke scrambled onto the bank, the unseen creature advanced on Artoo. Luke drew his blaster, but it was too late. Artoo had been swallowed by a dragonsnake.

Silence descended. Luke peered into the murk. With a screeching wail, Artoo was spat out, rocketing through the air and crashing through the foliage. Luke ran over, tipping Artoo upright. Then he sank down beside the droid. 'Artoo, what are we doing here?' he wondered hopelessly.

Concept art for the alien swamp creatures found on Dagobah.
RALPH MCQUARRIE

On the *Executor*, Admiral Piett entered Darth Vader's chamber and witnessed a sight few others had seen: the briefest glimpse of a scar-covered skull, before Vader's imposing helmet slid into place. The Dark Lord turned to hear the Admiral's report.

CINEMATIC CLASSICS

Concept art for Yoda, based on the original brief by George Lucas. **Joe Johnston**

Piett was reluctant to send more ships into the asteroid field after the *Millennium Falcon*, but Vader was adamant. 'I want that ship, not excuses.'

As night fell over Dagobah, Luke finished setting up camp. Suddenly, he felt a strange, watchful presence. He turned around, pointing his blaster at a small, green-skinned creature dressed in tattered robes.

'Away put your weapon!' the creature croaked. 'I mean you no harm!'

The creature hobbled into the camp, rifling through Luke's stores. He seemed fascinated by a small torch, but when Artoo tried to retrieve it, the creature whacked him with his walking stick. 'Mine!' he shouted. 'Mine! Mine!'

EPISODE V: THE EMPIRE STRIKES BACK

Concept art for Yoda. **Ralph McQuarrie**

Luke lost his patience, telling the creature he'd come a long way to find a Jedi Master. At this, the creature gave a gasp. 'Yoda,' he said. 'You seek Yoda.'

Luke crouched. 'You know him?' he asked in disbelief.

The creature nodded. 'Take you to him, I will,' he promised, shuffling away between the trees. Leaving Artoo to watch the camp, Luke reluctantly followed.

On the *Millennium Falcon*, the crew worked hard to fix the hyperdrive. In a secluded corridor, Leia was soldering when Han stepped in behind her and attempted to help. Leia shrugged him off, but deep down she knew she was developing feelings for the brash smuggler. Under Han's questioning, she grudgingly admitted that she liked him – but only when he wasn't acting like a scoundrel.

Han smiled, gently taking hold of her hands. 'You like me because I'm a scoundrel,' he said. 'There aren't enough scoundrels in your life.'

He leaned in for a kiss, and Leia kissed him back. But their passionate moment was short-lived, as Han was interrupted by a tap on the shoulder.

It was C-3PO, with an update on the repairs. Han thanked the droid sarcastically, and when he turned back, Leia had slipped away.

CINEMATIC CLASSICS

On the *Executor*, Darth Vader knelt before a holographic communication from his master, Emperor Palpatine, the supreme ruler of the galaxy. The Emperor had detected a disturbance in the Force and surmised that their new enemy, Luke Skywalker, was the offspring of Anakin Skywalker, a powerful Jedi.

'How is that possible?' Vader asked.

'Search your feelings, Lord Vader. You will know it to be true. He could destroy us,' the Emperor warned. 'The son of Skywalker must not become a Jedi.'

'If he could be turned,' Darth Vader suggested, 'he would become a powerful ally.'

The Emperor agreed. Vader promised, 'He will join us or die, Master.'

Concept art for Darth Vader communicating with a hologram of the Emperor. **Ralph McQuarrie**

EPISODE V: THE EMPIRE STRIKES BACK

In a tiny mud hut deep in the swamps of Dagobah, Luke Skywalker peppered his host with questions about Yoda. The ancient creature urged patience, offering Luke a bowl of stew and insisting that it wouldn't take long to reach the Jedi Master. But Luke couldn't sit still. 'We're wasting our time!' he snapped.

Yoda sighed, turning to the wall. 'I cannot teach him,' he said, seemingly to himself. 'The boy has no patience.'

Concept art for Yoda's home on Dagobah.
NORMAN REYNOLDS

'He will learn patience,' a voice replied, and Luke looked up in surprise. It was the voice of Obi-Wan Kenobi.

The little creature shook his head. 'Much anger in him. Like his father.'

'Yoda?' Luke realised. 'I am ready. I can be a Jedi.'

CINEMATIC CLASSICS

'Ready, are you? What know you of ready?' Yoda demanded. 'For 800 years have I trained Jedi. My own counsel will I keep on who is to be trained. A Jedi must have the deepest commitment. The most serious mind.'

He sighed. 'This one, a long time have I watched,' he went on. 'All his life has he looked away to the future, to the horizon. Never his mind on where he was. What he was doing. Adventure. Excitement. A Jedi craves not these things.'

Luke faced the aged warrior. 'I won't fail you,' he promised. 'I'm not afraid.'

Yoda's eyes narrowed. 'You will be,' he said ominously. 'You will be.'

In the cockpit of the *Millennium Falcon*, Princess Leia was lost in thought, listening to the distant boom of TIE bombers moving through the asteroid field. Suddenly, she saw a shape pass by, and a sticky sucker attached itself to the viewport.

She leapt up, hurrying to tell Han. He grabbed a breathing mask and set out to investigate. Leia and Chewie followed, descending the *Falcon*'s ramp into the interior of the cave. Fog covered the surface, and the ground was unusually soft and damp.

'I have a bad feeling about this,' Leia muttered.

There was a screech overhead, and Han fired his blaster. It was a mynock, a winged scavenger species known to attach themselves to starships.

Concept art of a mynock.
RALPH MCQUARRIE

EPISODE V: THE EMPIRE STRIKES BACK

A whole flock of the creatures screeched past, tangling in Chewie's fur. When the Wookiee fired his bowcaster, the entire cave shook. To confirm his unwelcome suspicion, Han fired his blaster into the ground. Again, the cave shuddered violently, almost throwing them off their feet as they staggered back to the *Falcon*.

'Let's get out of here!' Han cried. As the *Falcon* lifted off, they saw the tunnel collapsing ahead of them, huge stalactites and stalagmites seemingly coming together to block their escape. Han tipped the *Falcon* on its side and they slid through, right between the teeth of the giant space slug in whose belly they'd unwittingly been hiding. The massive creature snapped at the fleeing spacecraft, then retreated into its lair.

Concept art for the space slug creature, exogorth. **Joe Johnston**

CINEMATIC CLASSICS

On Dagobah, Luke's Jedi training had begun. For hours, he had undergone a series of punishing tasks, clambering up vines, swinging across fetid pools of water, leaping over roots and jogging through filthy bogs, all the while carrying Yoda on his back.

The Jedi Master warned Luke about the dark side of the Force – how seductive it was, and how easy it could be to give oneself over to anger, just as Obi-Wan's apprentice Darth Vader had. 'A Jedi uses the Force for knowledge and defence,' Yoda instructed. 'Never for attack.'

Concept art for Luke carrying Yoda on his back on Dagobah. RALPH MCQUARRIE

EPISODE V: THE EMPIRE STRIKES BACK

He climbed down, perching on a rock as Luke shivered, overtaken by a sudden sense of unease. 'There's something not right here,' he said. 'I feel cold.'

Yoda gestured to a dark opening between the roots of a great tree. He told Luke that it was a place of evil, strong with the dark side. And Luke would have to go inside.

'What's in there?' he asked doubtfully.

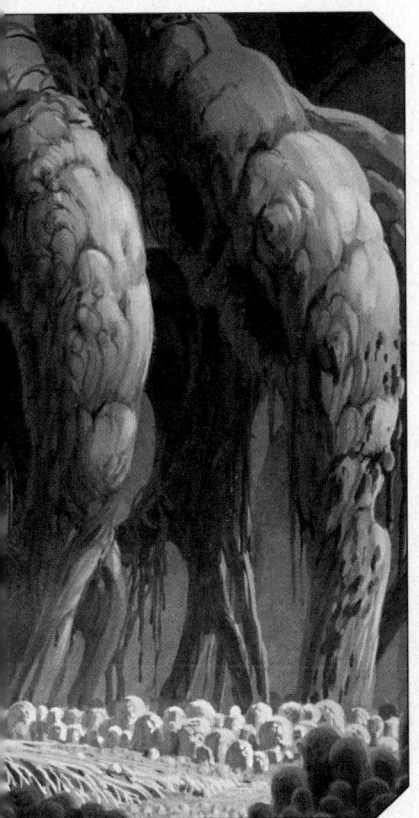

'Only what you take with you,' Yoda replied.

Luke approached the cave. Yoda urged him to leave his weapons behind but Luke didn't listen, buckling on his belt as he descended into the shadows. Then, he saw something impossible. From a stone tunnel emerged the unmistakable form of Darth Vader.

Luke ignited his lightsaber, and Vader did the same. Moving slowly, as though in a dream, Luke parried the Dark Lord's blow, then lunged in for the attack. His laser sword severed Vader's head from his shoulders, sending it tumbling into the dirt.

Luke looked down in amazement. In a shower of sparks, Vader's helmet split open, revealing the face beneath. Luke clutched his lightsaber. The face was his own.

CINEMATIC CLASSICS

On the bridge of the *Executor*, Imperial officers muttered in disgust. In an effort to track down the *Millennium Falcon*, Darth Vader had gathered a motley group of bounty hunters, some of the most feared and loathed creatures in the galaxy. Among them were notorious villains like the scaly reptilian Bossk, the assassin droid IG-88, the insectoid Zuckuss and the infamous Mandalorian warrior, Boba Fett.

Vader offered a substantial reward, and each of the mercenaries was determined to claim the prize. But just then, word came that an Imperial ship had caught sight of the *Falcon* and was already in pursuit.

Concept art for Boba Fett with fellow bounty hunters on Cloud City. **Ralph McQuarrie**

EPISODE V: THE EMPIRE STRIKES BACK

The *Millennium Falcon* emerged from the asteroid field, right into the path of a massive Star Destroyer. Once again, Han gave the order to jump to lightspeed, but once again, the hyperdrive failed. As blasts from the Star Destroyer rocked the ship, Threepio announced that the main rear deflector shield was now inoperative. Han had no choice but to turn the *Falcon* around and move into attack position.

On the Star Destroyer's bridge, the commanding officer, Captain Needa, watched in disbelief as the *Millennium Falcon* rocketed towards them. But as it passed overhead, the *Falcon* suddenly vanished from the Star Destroyer's scopes. The ship was gone.

On Dagobah, Luke was deep in concentration, balancing on one hand as he kept a small boulder suspended with the power of the Force. Yoda perched on the sole of Luke's foot, offering his young apprentice the benefit of his wisdom.

Concept art for Yoda's house, featuring Yoda and R2-D2.
NORMAN REYNOLDS

Suddenly Artoo began to beep worriedly, breaking Luke's focus and sending Yoda tumbling. Ever since they'd crash-landed on Dagobah, Luke's X-wing had been sinking deeper into the swamp. Now it was almost submerged.

CINEMATIC CLASSICS

'We'll never get it out now,' Luke complained.

'So certain are you,' Yoda told him. 'Always with you it cannot be done. Hear you nothing that I say?'

Luke turned to the X-wing. 'All right,' he said sceptically. 'I'll give it a try.'

'No!' Yoda ordered. 'Try not. Do. Or do not. There is no try.'

Raising his hand, Luke reached out with the Force, silently willing his ship to rise from the water. Yoda watched wide-eyed as the fighter's wing rose slowly from the murk. But then Luke lost his concentration.

'I can't,' he said. 'It's too big.'

Concept art for the head of an aging Yoda.
Ralph McQuarrie

'Size matters not,' Yoda told him. 'Look at me. Judge me by my size, do you? Hmm? And well you should not, for my ally is the Force, and a powerful ally it is. Life creates it, makes it grow. Its energy surrounds us, and binds us. Luminous beings are we, not this crude matter.'

EPISODE V: THE EMPIRE STRIKES BACK

Luke walked away, sinking to the ground in despair. He didn't see the old Jedi Master closing his eyes and reaching out. The waters of the swamp began to stir, and Artoo let out a startled beep as the X-wing lifted smoothly into the air, guided to dry land by an unseen power.

Luke hurried over, touching the hull of his ship in amazement. 'I don't believe it,' he told Yoda.

The little Jedi Master nodded. 'That is why you fail.'

Concept art storyboard for Yoda guiding Luke's X-wing to land on Dagobah. **JOE JOHNSTON**

On the *Executor*, Darth Vader stood over Captain Needa as the officer breathed his last. Then he turned to Admiral Piett, demanding an update on the missing *Falcon*. There had been no further sign of the ship, but Vader was not ready to give up the search. He ordered Piett to calculate every possible destination where the ship could be headed. 'Don't fail me again, Admiral,' he warned.

CINEMATIC CLASSICS

Little did they know that the *Millennium Falcon* hadn't escaped at all. The freighter clung to the back of the Star Destroyer's command tower, unseen by the rest of the fleet. Han was waiting for the larger ship to dump its garbage, then he'd detach the docking clamps and hide among the refuse.

'Then we gotta find a safe port somewhere around here,' he told Princess Leia. 'Any ideas?' Suddenly Han spotted something. 'This is interesting. Lando.'

Leia frowned. 'Lando system?'

'Lando's not a system, he's a man,' Solo explained. 'Lando Calrissian. He's a card player, gambler, scoundrel. You'd like him.'

'Can you trust him?' Leia asked.

'No,' Han admitted. 'But he's got no love for the Empire, I can tell you that. Here we go. Chewie, stand by. Detach.'

The *Falcon* dropped silently, tumbling to join the floating Imperial refuse. They waited until the fleet had gone to lightspeed. Then Han fired up the thrusters, piloting the *Falcon* away. He didn't notice the small stealth craft pursuing them.

Concept art for Boba Fett's starship. **NILO RODIS-JAMERO**

EPISODE V: THE EMPIRE STRIKES BACK

Concept art for Yoda preparing food at his stove for Luke. RALPH McQUARRIE

On Dagobah, Luke diligently continued his Jedi training as Yoda explained, 'Through the Force, things you will see. Other places. The future. The past. Old friends long gone.'

Luke reached out with his feelings, channelling the power of the Force. Suddenly, he felt a wave of horror pass through him. 'Han? Leia!'

His focus broke and he fell to the ground. He told Yoda about the vision he'd seen, of a city in the clouds and his friends in pain. 'Will they die?' Luke asked fearfully.

Yoda frowned. 'Difficult to see,' he admitted. 'Always in motion is the future.'

Luke began to gather his possessions. 'I've got to go to them.'

CINEMATIC CLASSICS

'Decide you must how to serve them best,' Yoda told him. 'If you leave now, help them you could. But you would destroy all for which they have fought and suffered.'

Light years away, Luke's vision was already coming true. The *Millennium Falcon* soared towards Cloud City, a mining colony suspended above the gas planet Bespin. Flanked by a pair of twin-pod cloud cars, the *Falcon* was granted permission to land. But when Han lowered the ramp, they found the landing platform deserted. 'I don't like this,' Leia said.

Concept art for Cloud City, featuring cloud cars and flying beasts in the sky. **Ralph McQuarrie**

EPISODE V: THE EMPIRE STRIKES BACK

With a hiss, a set of doors opened, and a cloaked figure strode towards them, accompanied by his guards. Lando Calrissian frowned as he spotted his old partner in crime, Han Solo. 'Why, you slimy, double-crossing, no-good swindler,' he growled. 'You've got a lot of guts coming here, after what you pulled.'

Then his face broke into a grin, and he laughed, pulling Han in for an embrace. 'How you doing, you old pirate? So good to see you!'

C-3PO watched with relief. 'Well, he seems very friendly.'

But Leia wasn't convinced. She eyed Lando as he reached for her hand, kissing her fingers. 'All right, you old smoothie,' Han cautioned. He knew his friend's reputation.

As they made their way through Cloud City, Lando told them all about the challenges of running a successful mining operation. 'You sound like a businessman.' Han laughed. 'A responsible leader. Who'd have thought that, huh?'

Threepio lagged behind when he heard a familiar beeping through an open door. 'That sounds like an Artoo unit in there,' he said, stepping through. But when a voice demanded to know who he was, Threepio backed up in surprise. Before he could explain, a blaster shot rang out and the golden droid was blown to pieces.

CINEMATIC CLASSICS

On Dagobah, Luke had readied his X-wing and was preparing to leave. Yoda beseeched the young man to stay and complete his training, but Luke was convinced that Han and Leia would die if he didn't help them. 'Master Yoda, I promise to return and finish what I've begun,' he said. 'You have my word.'

'Luke,' another voice called. The shimmering form of Obi-Wan Kenobi had appeared beside Yoda. 'I don't want to lose you to the Emperor, the way I lost Vader.'

'You won't,' Luke swore. Then he boarded his X-wing and fired up the engines.

Concept art for Luke Skywalker, Yoda and the ghost of Obi-Wan on Dagobah with the X-wing.
RALPH MCQUARRIE

EPISODE V: THE EMPIRE STRIKES BACK

Yoda and Obi-Wan watched regretfully as the ship blasted free of Dagobah's atmosphere. 'That boy is our last hope,' Kenobi said.

'No,' Yoda reminded him. 'There is another.'

Down in the furnace-lit depths of Cloud City, Chewbacca searched for C-3PO. The Wookiee was rifling through a scrap pile when he came across the golden droid's torso – and nearby, his detached head. Bellowing at the Ugnaught workers, Chewie gathered up all the pieces he could find.

Back in the guest quarters, Han and Leia were dismayed when Chewie showed them Threepio's sad state – the droid's parts collected in a crate. Just then, Lando entered, smiling appreciatively at Leia. 'You look absolutely beautiful,' he told her. 'You truly belong here with us, among the clouds. Would you join me for a little refreshment? Everyone's invited, of course.'

Concept art for Leia, Han Solo and Chewbacca – holding C-3PO – in Cloud City.
RALPH MCQUARRIE

CINEMATIC CLASSICS

As they made their way through the bustling corridors, Lando explained that although his operation was small, he'd been afraid that sooner or later the Empire would notice and close it down. 'But things have developed that'll ensure security,' he said. 'I've just made a deal that'll keep the Empire out of here forever.'

Concept art for Darth Vader and Lando Calrissian with Leia, Han Solo and Chewbacca in Vader's dining room on Cloud City. **Ralph McQuarrie**

EPISODE V: THE EMPIRE STRIKES BACK

He touched a button, and a door opened onto a white room with a long dining table. At the far end, a dark figure rose to his feet – it was Darth Vader. Han drew his blaster and fired, but Darth Vader simply raised a hand, deflecting the laser bolts. From an alcove stepped the bounty hunter, Boba Fett.

Vader beckoned. 'We would be honoured if you would join us.'

Chewbacca was taken to a cell, where a piercing alarm was agony to his sensitive Wookiee ears. When the alarm finally switched off, Chewie worried about Han and the Princess. Powerless to do anything else, he got to work repairing C-3PO.

In another part of Cloud City, Darth Vader watched with a pitiless gaze as Han Solo was strapped to a sparking electronic device. He emerged from the chamber, engaging Boba Fett. He promised the bounty hunter could take Solo to Jabba the Hutt once Luke Skywalker was in Imperial custody. Leia and Chewbacca would have to remain in Cloud City, as Lando's prisoners.

CINEMATIC CLASSICS

A costume concept for Lando Calrissian. RALPH MCQUARRIE

'That was never a condition of our agreement,' Lando protested. 'Nor was giving Han to this bounty hunter.'

Vader turned on him. 'Perhaps you think you're being treated unfairly?'

Lando gulped. He couldn't defy the Dark Lord. But as he walked away, Lando leaned closer to his aide, Lobot. 'This deal is getting worse all the time,' he muttered.

Back in the cell, Chewbacca had reattached C-3PO's head to his body. As Chewie continued tinkering, the droid's optical sensors reactivated and he realised his head was the wrong way round. 'What have you done?' Threepio wailed. 'I'm backwards!'

The door slid open, and stormtroopers brought in Han, who collapsed to the floor. As Chewie helped Han to a bench, guards shoved Leia into the cell. She knelt beside Han, gently stroking his hair. 'Why are they doing this?' she asked weakly.

— 52 —

EPISODE V: THE EMPIRE STRIKES BACK

Han couldn't answer. 'They never even asked me any questions.'

Two guards entered, followed closely by Lando Calrissian. He told them he was sorry, but insisted he'd had no choice – he couldn't jeopardize the entire population of Cloud City. 'Vader doesn't want you at all,' he explained. 'He's after somebody called Skywalker.'

Finally, Han and Leia understood. Vader was using them as bait to lure Luke into his trap. Lunging to his feet, Han punched Lando square on the jaw. Chewie roared as the guards drew their blasters, but Lando ordered them to stand down. He apologised again, then marched from the cell.

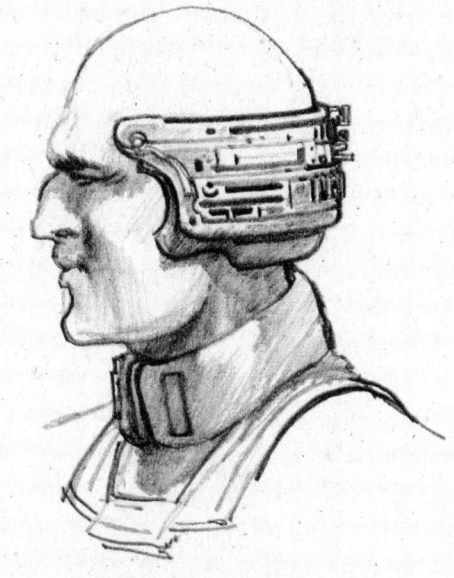

A costume concept for Lobot's headgear. **RALPH MCQUARRIE**

As Luke's X-wing approached Cloud City, Darth Vader instructed his men to allow the craft to land. He planned to subject Luke to a process known as carbon freezing, keeping him in suspended animation until he could be delivered to the Emperor. But the process was risky, so Vader decided to test it first – on Han Solo.

Han and the others were marched into the carbon freezing chamber. Chewbacca carried C-3PO's parts in a cargo net strapped to his back. The partially assembled droid complained and nattered during the tense proceedings.

When Vader gave the order to place Han into the carbon freezing device, Chewbacca gave a roar, knocking several stormtroopers off their feet. Han reached for his friend, urging him to save his strength. This time, they were outnumbered. But their chance would come again. For now, it was the Wookiee's responsibility to watch over the Princess.

Leia looked up at Han, deep emotion in her eyes. When he leaned in to kiss her, she returned his kiss. Then a pair of stormtroopers stepped in, dragging Han back.

'I love you,' Leia called out.

'I know,' Han replied.

Concept art for Han Solo in custody on Cloud City, featuring Darth Vader and his guards. RALPH MCQUARRIE

EPISODE V: THE EMPIRE STRIKES BACK

Then the platform he was standing on began to descend. Dense clouds erupted from the carbon freezing machine, enveloping Han in a shroud of steam. Chewie gave a howl of despair. Leia turned her face away.

Then a giant claw lowered, latching onto a slab of black carbonite. As it dropped to the floor, Leia saw the frozen outline of Han Solo, his mouth open in a wordless cry. He was still alive, and in perfect hibernation.

'He's all yours, bounty hunter,' Vader said. 'Reset the chamber for Skywalker.'

Concept art for the carbon freezing chamber. **NORMAN REYNOLDS**

The Dark Lord then ordered Lando to deliver Leia and Chewbacca to his ship. 'I'm altering the deal,' he told Calrissian. 'Pray I don't alter it any further.'

Luke and Artoo entered Cloud City, only to find its white corridors curiously empty. Suddenly, a blaster shot rang out. Taking cover, Luke saw a platoon of stormtroopers. With them were Leia, Chewie and Lando.

'Luke, don't!' Leia cried. 'It's a trap!' Then a door slid shut and they were gone.

CINEMATIC CLASSICS

As Luke tried to follow, he soon realised that Leia was right. One door cut him off from R2-D2, while a rising hatchway led him directly into the carbon freezing chamber. There he found a familiar figure waiting for him.

'The Force is with you, young Skywalker,' Darth Vader said, his voice echoing through the chamber. 'But you are not a Jedi yet.'

Concept art for Luke in the freezing plant on Cloud City. RALPH MCQUARRIE

EPISODE V: THE EMPIRE STRIKES BACK

As he approached, Luke drew his lightsaber, and Vader did the same. Luke struck first but Vader blocked easily, throwing Luke off his feet. Luke soon recovered and rejoined the fight.

Elsewhere in Cloud City, Lando had sprung a trap of his own. Led by Lobot, his guards disarmed the stormtroopers surrounding Leia and

CINEMATIC CLASSICS

Chewbacca. But when Lando removed the Wookiee's cuffs, Chewie grabbed him by the neck, throttling him.

'There's still a chance to save Han,' Lando wheezed desperately. 'At the east... platform...'

Concept art for two stormtroopers carrying Han aboard Boba Fett's starship. **Joe Johnston**

On Leia's order, Chewbacca released his grip. When they arrived at the landing platform, they saw Boba Fett's ship already lifting off. Leia fired at the departing craft, but it was no use. Han was gone.

In the carbon freezing chamber, Darth Vader had Luke cornered. When the young Jedi missed his step and tumbled into the carbon freezer, Vader thought his work was done. Luke quickly leapt free, retrieving his lightsaber and igniting it.

EPISODE V: THE EMPIRE STRIKES BACK

'Impressive,' Vader admitted. 'Most impressive. Obi-Wan has taught you well. You have controlled your fear. Now, release your anger. Only your hatred can destroy me.'

Luke attacked again, taking Vader by surprise and driving the Dark Lord down. Moving in pursuit, Luke found himself in a passage beneath the freezing chamber, where a circular window looked out over Cloud City's central air shaft.

Using the Force, Vader lifted a steel container and sent it hurtling towards Luke. More heavy objects followed, slamming painfully into Luke and then past him to the window, shattering the glass. A fierce wind tore through the passage, dragging Luke through the broken window. Exhausted, he managed to cling to a metal gantry. Below him was nothing but a sheer drop.

A costume concept for Darth Vader. RALPH MCQUARRIE

Knowing Cloud City was no longer safe, Lando made an announcement, telling his people to evacuate before more Imperial troops arrived. Citizens crowded the corridors, carrying whatever they could. Lando led Leia and the others to the *Millennium Falcon*'s landing platform, and R2-D2 provided a cloud of smoke to cover their escape. Under heavy fire from pursuing stormtroopers, they fled to the ship, lifting off into the skies above Bespin.

CINEMATIC CLASSICS

Meanwhile, Luke had clawed his way up onto the metal gantry only to come face to face with Darth Vader. Their lightsabers clashed but now Luke was bruised and weary, his blows weakening as Vader drove him back. Finally, he stumbled, toppling back as Vader loomed over him. 'You are beaten,' the Dark Lord said. 'It is useless to resist. Don't let yourself be destroyed as Obi-Wan did.'

Concept art for Luke Skywalker's battle with Vader in Cloud City on Bespin. **Ralph McQuarrie**

EPISODE V: THE EMPIRE STRIKES BACK

With a last effort of will, Luke rose up and kept fighting, but a savage blow from Vader ended the battle, severing Luke's hand and sending his lightsaber tumbling into the air shaft. Luke screamed, clutching his cauterised wound. Vader faced him, reaching out a gloved hand. He urged Luke to join him, and together they could bring order to the galaxy.

'I'll never join you!' Luke cried.

'If you only knew the power of the dark side!' Vader insisted. 'Obi-Wan never told you what happened to your father.'

'He told me enough,' Luke rasped defiantly. 'He told me you killed him.'

'No,' Vader said. '*I* am your father.'

Luke shook his head. It couldn't be possible. Vader urged the young Jedi to search his feelings, to recognise the truth. 'Join me,' he repeated, 'and together we can rule the galaxy as father and son.'

But Luke refused to surrender. Instead he let go of the gantry, dropping down the seemingly endless shaft. Vader could only watch as Luke vanished from sight.

The air shaft narrowed, and Luke found himself sliding helplessly through a tunnel before plummeting through an open hatch. He clung to a slender vane high above the gas clouds as the wind lashed at him. Luke closed his eyes and reached out with the Force. 'Leia,' he whispered. 'Hear me. Leia.'

In the cockpit of the *Falcon*, Leia felt something pass through her. 'Luke,' she whispered.

CINEMATIC CLASSICS

Concept art for Luke clutching onto the weather vane. RALPH MCQUARRIE

Turning to Chewbacca, she gave the order to return to Cloud City. As they sped closer, Lando spotted someone dangling from the city's underbelly. Opening the top hatch, he retrieved Luke and carried him safely back into the ship. Pursued by a trio of TIE fighters, the *Falcon* soared into open space.

But their troubles weren't over. As Chewie struggled to evade the fighters, Leia spotted the *Executor* moving to cut off their escape. And when Lando gave the order to jump to lightspeed, they discovered that the hyperdrive had been deactivated by Imperial forces.

On the *Executor*'s bridge, Darth Vader received a report that the *Falcon* would soon be in range of their tractor beam. He could sense Luke's presence aboard the ship and was determined not to let him escape again. Luke, too, could feel the Dark Lord calling to him. He didn't know if he was strong enough to resist.

EPISODE V: THE EMPIRE STRIKES BACK

In the *Falcon*'s hold, R2-D2 was communicating with the ship's computer. Using his robotic arm, the astromech was able to repair the fault in the hyperdrive. The ship suddenly burst into lightspeed, sending the little droid tumbling. In the cockpit, Luke and the others saw the stars blur into streaks of light.

On the bridge of the *Executor*, Admiral Piett watched fearfully as Darth Vader turned and marched wordlessly away.

The Rebel fleet glided through space, a majestic flotilla of fighters and attack craft – yet still no match for the might of the Empire. Aboard the *Millennium Falcon*, Lando and Chewbacca were preparing to leave on a mission to rescue Han Solo.

On the frigate *Nebulon-B*, Luke was fitted with an artificial hand. 'I'll meet you at the rendezvous point on Tatooine,' he told Lando over the comlink.

Then Luke walked over to Leia and put his arm around her shoulders. R2-D2 and C-3PO, now fully repaired and functional, joined the Jedi and the Princess. Together, they gazed out of the viewport as the *Falcon* moved away from the fleet. They had suffered many defeats at the hands of the Empire, and the battle to free the galaxy from tyranny was still far from over.

Concept art for Leia embracing Luke.
RALPH MCQUARRIE

CINEMATIC CLASSICS

Artists

Concept art for Rebel snowspeeders surrounding an Imperial AT-AT during the Battle of Hoth.
RALPH McQUARRIE

RALPH MCQUARRIE, born in Indiana in 1929, was a legend in the field of conceptual illustration. McQuarrie produced concept paintings for *E.T.: The Extra-Terrestrial*, the original *Battlestar Galactica* television series, all three films in the classic *Star Wars* trilogy, and the movie *Cocoon*, for which he won an Academy Award for Visual Effects. Prior to his career in film production, McQuarrie worked as a technical illustrator at Boeing. After partnering with young filmmaker George Lucas, he painted scenes from Lucas's second draft script that informed the design direction of the film. In doing so he helped create some of the most iconic characters in

EPISODE V: THE EMPIRE STRIKES BACK

movie history, including C-3PO, R2-D2, and Darth Vader. McQuarrie's paintings have been reproduced as collectible posters and prints, and his original artworks have appeared in museum exhibitions, including the wildly popular touring show *Star Wars: The Magic of Myth*. He passed away in 2012.

TERRY CHOSTNER joined Industrial Light & Magic in 1979 as a still photographer in the miniatures unit on *The Empire Strikes Back*. Other early projects included *Poltergeist*, *Return of the Jedi*, *Indiana Jones and the Temple of Doom*, *The Abyss*, *Terminator 2: Judgment Day*, and *Jurassic Park*. With the emergence of computer graphics techniques, Chostner later became a matchmove and digital artist, working on films like *Star Wars: Attack of the Clones*, *Transformers*, *Iron Man*, and *Star Trek*. He passed away in 2019.

NORMAN REYNOLDS was a British production designer and art director who worked on the original *Star Wars* trilogy. He art directed *Star Wars*, for which he won his first Academy Award for Best Art Direction – a category later renamed as Best Production Design. He also worked as the production designer for *The Empire Strikes Back* and *Return of the Jedi*. Reynolds won his second Academy Award and a BAFTA Award for his work on *Raiders of the Lost Ark* (1981). He passed away in 2023.

DENNIS MUREN is an American visual effects artist and supervisor and nine-time Academy Award winner. Hailed as a pioneer of visual effects, he has worked with directors George Lucas, Steven Spielberg and James Cameron and lended his talents to *Star Wars*, *E.T. the Extra Terrestrial* (1982), *Indiana Jones and the Temple of Doom* (1984) and many more films. He worked as a visual effects cameraman on *Star Wars*, before being promoted to visual effects director of photography for *The Empire Strikes Back*. He worked with Lucas as creative consultant on *A Force Awakens* (2015) and continues to make cinematic masterpieces.

CINEMATIC CLASSICS

Concept art for snowtroopers loading AT-AT walkers on Hoth. JOE JOHNSTON

EPISODE V: THE EMPIRE STRIKES BACK

JOE JOHNSTON is an award-winning film director and effects artist whose directorial career includes classics such as *Honey, I Shrunk the Kids*; *The Rocketeer*; *Jumanji*; *October Sky*; and *Captain America: The First Avenger*. Born in Austin, Texas, Johnston attended California State University Long Beach and the Art Center College of Design before working as a storyboard artist and special effects art director on the first *Star Wars* trilogy. At Lucasfilm, Johnston worked closely with George Lucas to develop designs for now-iconic vehicles and characters and wrote a children's book starring the Ewoks from *Return of the Jedi*. After the *Star Wars* trilogy wrapped, Johnston attended the University of Southern California film school as a step toward developing his own directorial skills and served as associate producer on George Lucas's 1988 film *Willow*. Johnston, who won an Academy Award for Best Visual Effects for his work on *Raiders of the Lost Ark*, has continued his moviemaking career as director of the 2013 thriller *Not Safe for Work*.

NILO RODIS-JAMERO is a producer and production designer who was born in the Phillipines. He worked as assistant art director of visual effects on *The Empire Strikes Back*, returning to the *Star Wars* saga as costume designer for *Return of the Jedi*. His filmography includes *Raiders of the Lost Ark* (1981), *Poltergeist* (1982), *Star Trek III: The Search for Spock* (1984) and *Star Trek IV: The Voyage Home* (1986). He is credited for art direction on Tim Burton's *Alice in Wonderland* (2010).

CINEMATIC CLASSICS

Concept art for Leia and Chewie firing at Boba Fett as he escapes from Cloud City.
RALPH MCQUARRIE

EPISODE V: THE EMPIRE STRIKES BACK

ACKNOWLEDGEMENTS

The author warmly thanks Nigel Thornton for making his photographic collection available; in particular his interior shots of the Compiegne greatly enhance the finished publication. Phll Neumann is also gratefully thanked for allowing access to the extensive FotoFlite collection at Ashford and locating some excellent images which have not been previously published. Finally to my colleague Miles Cowsill, my thanks for designing the book and making the project possible.

CONTENTS

Introduction 4

1   The Dieppe Years 8

2   The Dunkirk Years 34

3   The Calais Years 44

Fleet List 106

Produced and designed by Ferry Publications trading as Lily Publications Ltd

PO Box 33, Ramsey, Isle of Man, British Isles, IM99 4LP

Tel: +44 (0) 1624 898446   Fax: +44 (0) 1624 898449

www.ferrypubs.co.uk   E-Mail: info@lilypublications.co.uk

Printed and bound by Gomer Press Ltd., Wales, UK +44 (0) 1559 362371 © Lily Publications 2013

First Published: August 2013

All rights reserved. No part of this book or any of the photographs may be reproduced or transmitted in any form or by any means, electronic or mechanical, including photocopying, recording or by any means of information storage and retrieval system without written permission from the publisher, save only for brief extracts which may be used solely for the purpose of review.

INTRODUCTION

In the early years of steam navigation between the UK and France, the construction of railways between London, Paris and the English Channel ports was vital for speeding up the through services between capitals. Inevitably the majority of railway companies also became ship owners and ports and harbours were extended, dredged and deepened to accommodate larger and improved tonnage.

The railway system in France developed in a quite different way to that in Britain. Here private enterprise very much led the growth of the Victorian network with minimal government interference whereas in France it was the state that built the majority of the system and then invited private companies to operate the lines under leases of up to 99 years. The state guaranteed the dividends of the railway companies and in turn took two-thirds of the profits.

Eventually six large companies operated the lines radiating outwards from Paris, the Chemin de Fer du Nord heading towards Picardy and its ports of Dunkirk, Calais, Boulogne and the Chemins de Fer de l'Ouest to the Normandy port of Dieppe which was opened in August 1848. The Ouest was taken over by the Chemin de Fer de l'Etat in 1909.

By 1850, each of the three northern ports found itself at the end of quite separate branch lines which were opened in the late 1840s, Calais and Dunkirk being reached via Lille and a common junction at Hazebrouck. The line to Boulogne was via Amiens and Abbeville but it was to be another 20 years before a direct line between Calais and Boulogne was opened over the Caffiers Marquise summit. The completion of this demanding section with its steep gradients cut 30

The **SeaFrance Moliere** proved to be the company's final acquisition and one which they could ill afford. (John Hendy)

minutes from the train journey between Calais and Paris and became the principal route for the boat trains linking the UK and French capital cities.

Competition from road transport during the 1930s saw a huge reduction in the French national railway network. The financial problems faced by the railway companies finally saw their complete nationalisation as from 1st January 1938 when the Societe Nationale des Chemins de Fer Francais (herein after referred to as SNCF) was formed.

By the mid-1960s, the nature of cross-Channel trade was dramatically changing by the acceptance of roll on – roll off lorry traffic and what had been a seasonal business carrying tourist cars grew into the year-round industry we see today. This period also saw a huge growth in car ownership and rather than take the train, year-round motoring holidays

THE SeaFrance YEARS

The turbine passenger steamer **Cote d'Azur** *(II) maintained the Calais – Folkestone route until she was withdrawn in September 1972. (FotoFlite)*

became the norm. Trains were frequently perceived as dirty and old fashioned and lacked the flexibility provided by the motorcar.

For many established 'railway' ports, the introduction of the new trade was to become their downfall. Whereas they were generally suited to the transfer of passengers and cargo which had arrived by Victorian railway, at this time the road systems had not evolved to the same extent and often involved vehicle traffic passing through narrow streets in urban centres on its way to the nearby docks. Thus Newhaven and Folkestone would not develop in the same way as Dover or Calais for which new by-pass roads were constructed leading the speeding traffic flows away from the centres of population. Although new more convenient ports were eventually built at Dieppe and Boulogne, neither arrived early

Towards the end of her career, the first French car ferry **Compiegne** *was relegated to the secondary Dover-Boulogne link. The stern loader is seen alongside at berth 13 at the Gare Maritime. (Miles Cowsill)*

1 Chapter Title

enough to save them from decline. The motorway system radiating from Calais proved so efficient that in terms of travel time, there was now no longer anything to be gained by using the longer sea routes.

This publication seeks to trace the post Second World War development of the ships and English Channel routes with which SNCF was involved and in particular, its subsidiary company SeaFrance on the Calais – Dover Short-Sea link. Poor operational performance and constant strikes made the Dieppe – Newhaven route the least reliable crossing in NW Europe and led to its inevitable demise before brief revivals by Stena Line, Hoverspeed and the present truncated service offered by Transmanche Ferries.

Sadly, the Calais – Dover crossing was not to learn from the errors made in the Normandy port and followed a similar destructive path leading to the eventual and tragic liquidation of SeaFrance. The situation was not helped by the management's failure to supply the route with the right ships to compete in an ever-challenging market place. The *SeaFrance Moliere* was the ship that sank SeaFrance, plunging the company into even greater debt at a time when it should have been concentrating on the consolidation of an already precarious trading position.

But during its period of operation, SeaFrance and its predecessors provided the cross-Channel traveller with much for which we can be thankful. They were responsible for many new innovations, both technical and architectural which rival companies were keen to follow. The French supplied the Channel with some magnificent ships which were always in the state of the art category. Passengers knew that they were in France as soon as they stepped on board in Dover, Folkestone or Newhaven and the ships literally appealed to all the senses, not least in the gastronomic field.

The part played by SeaFrance and its forebears in the English Channel trades is for the first time presented in book form. The company's achievements are history but its legacy lives on.

John Hendy
Ivychurch
Kent
August 2013

The **Cote d'Azur** (III) is seen off Folkestone awaiting berthing trials on 29th September 1981 as the Sealink UK vessel **Horsa** clears the harbour pier bound for Boulogne. (FotoFlite)

CHAPTER I

The Dieppe Years

THE SeaFrance YEARS

The historic Newhaven – Dieppe service was two-thirds French owned and had been ever since 1862 when the London Brighton & South Coast Railway entered into a working agreement with the Chemins de Fer de l'Ouest. The exact fraction was 37/56ths and was based on the length of the railway journeys from the ports to their respective capitals. In essence this meant that two-thirds of every ship and two-thirds of all revenues passed to the French railway company, a state of affairs which was later to cause serious obstacles to the further development of the route.

POST-WAR REVIVAL

The Second World War had seen the significant losses of the British steamers *Paris* (1913) and *Brighton* (1933) while the French-crewed *Newhaven* and *Rouen* (1912) and the *Versailles* (1921) were not considered worth reconditioning at the war's end.

Prior to the start of hostilities, an order had been placed at Le Havre for replacements for the 1912 sisters. Originally to be named *Dieppe* and *Newhaven* their names were changed to *Londres* and *Vichy* before the former was seized on the stocks by the invading German army and eventually used as the coastal minelayer *Lothringen*. At the end of the war she was returned to Le Havre and entered service at Dieppe during April 1947. The sister ship was eventually named *Arromanches*, after the Normandy invasion beach, and entered service in summer 1947.

Meanwhile the railways in Britain were nationalised in 1948 and the sole survivor of the pre-war fleets was the 1928-built *Worthing*, the sister ship to the *Brighton* which had been lost at Dieppe in 1940. British Railways went back to Denny of Dumbarton for a replacement and the new *Brighton* (the sixth ship to carry that name) entered service in 1950. The vessel was a smaller but faster version of the Dover Strait steamer *Maid of Orleans* which Denny had built in the previous year. In the following year, SNCF returned to Le Havre builders Forges et Cie de la Mediterranee for the *Lisieux* of 1953. She was very much a smaller version of the *Cote d'Azur* which had been built by the same yard for the Calais – Folkestone crossing in August 1950. It can be seen that the new ships very much followed the trend of steamers on the route which required a shorter length in order to manoeuvre with ease within the confines of the River Ouse at Newhaven and the inner port at Dieppe.

The arrival on station of the *Lisieux* allowed British Railways to withdraw the pre-war steamer *Worthing* in May 1955 at which time SNCF transferred the ownership of the *Londres* which raised the Red Ensign and worked with a British crew ensuring that both partners supplied the Newhaven – Dieppe route with two ships. However, in addition to the four passenger steamers, SNCF also provided the three identical cargo vessels *Brest*, *Nantes* and *Rennes* in which increasing numbers of cars were crane loaded and shipped across the Channel while motorists travelled in the

Alongside at Dieppe during the 50s are the **Arromanches**, **Lisieux** *and the cargo vessel* **Rennes**. *(Ferry Publications Library)*

1 The Dieppe Years

The **Worthing** is seen leaving Dieppe shortly before her withdrawal at the end of the 1954 season. (Ferry Publications Library)

The **Brighton** (VI) leaves Dieppe in July 1962. (Henry Maxwell)

conventional steamer leaving port an hour later. Each of these motor vessels had a capacity for as many as 60 cars.

By 1960, the route had reached a stage in its development which demanded change. Annual passenger numbers using the route had declined by 29 per cent since 1955 whereas on the Short-Sea routes at Dover and Folkestone, they had risen by 34 per cent during the same period. Admittedly, some of this trend could be attributed to the fact that since 1956, the Dieppe – Newhaven crossing had become seasonal with the ships laid up between the end of October and the following Easter. However, the passenger steamers were (until March 1964) two-class vessels which required the duplication of all on-board facilities and added to this, their fast crossing times and fuel-thirsty engines meant that in a changing world they were never going to be economical ships to operate. The four steam ships were built to carry train-connected passengers to and from London and Paris via the most direct route between the capital cities. Yet at the same time when year on year, the number of motorists using the route was showing a marked increase, the percentage of foot passengers using boat trains was sharply dropping.

ENTER THE FALAISE

It was not surprising that the route's saviour was the long-awaited introduction of a car ferry. This was the versatile former Southern Railway Southampton steamer *Falaise* which had been built by Denny's in 1947 mainly for the seasonal St Malo route although she also saw work both on the Le Havre and Channel Islands links. It was stated at her launch that she was 'intended primarily for the Channel Islands traffic but that she can also be used on the Dover, Folkestone and Newhaven services and short-sea cruises' and so the Southern had seen her very much as, what became known later, an 'inter-available' vessel. At the end of her first season, she had even briefly deputised on the legendary Dover – Calais 'Golden Arrow' crossing for a period of one month, a schedule which was repeated in the following year.

British Railways had been seeking to close their loss-making Le Havre and St Malo routes for some years and after permission had finally been granted, the Le Havre steamer *Normannia* and the 17-year-old *Falaise* were sent to the Tyne for conversion to car ferries. The *Falaise* left Southampton for Vickers Armstrong (Shipbuilders) Ltd on 4th January 1964.

Top left: The **Lisieux** alongside at Newhaven. (Ferry Publications Library)

Top right: The cargo vessel **Nantes** leaves Dieppe for Newhaven in July 1963. (Henry Maxwell)

Left: The **Brighton** (VI) swings in the inner harbour at Dieppe prior to her departure for Newhaven in July 1962. Both she and the **Lisieux** closed the daily passenger service on 25th May 1965. (Henry Maxwell)

Above: Seen during her first season as a car ferry, the **Falaise** appeared in a rather clumsy livery that was thankfully modified for the 1965 season. (Ferry Publications Library)

1 The Dieppe Years

The **Arromanches** of 1946 is seen at speed on passage to Newhaven. (FotoFlite)

The two-class ship, with accommodation for 1,527 passengers and sleeping berths for 338, was totally gutted and transformed, re-emerging with a passenger certificate for 700 one-class passengers and a split-level garage capable of carrying 100 cars (75 on the Main Deck and 25 on the Mezzanine Deck above). If required, four lorries could be accommodated adjacent to her stern door which reduced the car numbers to just 80.

The first car ferry to test the Newhaven and Dieppe linkspans was the Calais vessel Compiegne which was sent for trials early in 1964. Although she negotiated the River Ouse at Newhaven without problem, it was seen that berthing at Dieppe might cause her future difficulties.

After an inaugural excursion on Sunday 31st May 1964, the Falaise commenced commercial service at 10.00 on the following day reintroducing year-round schedules on the link.

The passenger steamer Londres had been withdrawn from service at the close of her 1963 season and soon passed to Greek owners while her French sister ship Arromanches followed suit in 1964. The newer Lisieux and Brighton continued to operate although their days were certainly numbered, particularly when in May 1964 SNCF ordered twin car ferries for the following season.

If British Railways and SNCF had ever had any doubts concerning the future of the Newhaven – Dieppe crossing, these were immediately extinguished by the unrivalled success of the new service. In 1963 fewer than 35,000 cars had used the route via the old lift on – lift off method. During the first year of the Falaise, the number rose to over 83,000 and in 1965 (the first year of the new French car ferries) to just over 175,000. During the same three years, the percentage of foot passengers arriving on Boat Trains dropped from almost 74 per cent to 42 per cent and continued to fall throughout the decade while overall passenger numbers continued to show a healthy increase.

TWIN FERRIES FOR SNCF

The first of the new £1.6 million SNCF ferries was launched at Nantes during November 1964 and named *Villandry* while her sister, *Valencay*, entered the water at St Nazaire in the following February.

Prior to their arrival, the service had experienced some difficulties with the *Falaise* hitting the pier at Dieppe in August 1964 and again at Newhaven during October. The *Normannia* from Dover was called in to deputise and thereafter became a regular visitor. During gales at Easter 1965, the *Falaise* managed to hit the East Pier at Newhaven causing considerable damage to her bow. Initially cars were once again crane loaded onto passenger ships before all vehicle traffic was re-routed via Dover. Two days later, the *Normannia* was hurriedly despatched westwards and took up service in place of the stricken car ferry.

The new *Villandry* arrived at Newhaven on her inaugural voyage on 16th May 1965, officially opening the new £330,000 terminal, but did not take up commercial crossings until 30th May. The remaining two passenger steamers continued in service with the *Brighton* operating 'no passport' excursions at weekends allowing seven-hours ashore for just 47/6d (£2.37). However, with the impending arrival of the *Valencay*, the *Lisieux* was withdrawn from service on 26th June and was chartered to the French Line (CGT) in the following month for a series of excursions running between St Malo and Jersey with a weekly connection to Torquay and later Weymouth. The service ended in September before the 12-year-old ship was offered for sale, passing to Greek owners Agapitos in the following March for £240,000.

The *Valencay* duly commenced service on 7th July 1965

This 1972 view of the Falaise berthing at Newhaven also shows the port's original rail/ship interchange. (John Hendy)

after which the smaller *Falaise* was switched to off-peak sailings.

Aesthetically, the new French twins bore certain similarities to the Calais – Dover car ferry *Compiegne* of 1958 and had continued the 45-degree drop in black hull paint below the foremast as introduced to SNCF by the Danish-built *Saint-Germain* in 1951. Following her conversion in 1964, the *Falaise* had spent her first season as a car ferry looking very bottom heavy with the line of the hull paint continuing aft in a straight line between her high fo'c'sle and stern. Happily, the introduction of her new French running partners saw this rather clumsy application modified and there is little doubt that the ship always looked far better in this guise.

The *Villandry* and *Valencay* were the first diesel-engined passenger ships on the route and also introduced other innovations which were to become commonplace. They were fitted with controllable pitched propellers which gave them

The **Villandry** of 1965 was one of a pair of French motor vessels that completely transformed the route's fortunes. (FotoFlite)

the required thrust by changing the angle of the blades which were in constant motion and were controlled from the bridge by the Master. Twin rudders helped give the ships far greater manoeuvrability and the fitting of bow-thrust units eased the ships' bows on and off their quays. Stern docking bridges were also fitted although these were little used and subsequently removed.

With capacity for as many as 1,200 passengers and 150 cars, the twin ferries were purely stern loaders and as they were built to replace three conventional cargo vessels, they also handled general cargo loaded by BR Brute design trolleys which were towed on board by battery-electric tractors. Passenger luggage was also stored on the vehicle decks in tractor-driven luggage cages which saved the ships' public spaces from becoming clogged with baggage.

Looking to make savings in fuel, the crossing time was expanded to 3 hours 45 minutes and each ship managed two round crossings each day which were no longer timed to especially coincide with convenient rail departure times from London or Paris.

With the motorists' service now up and running, the *Villandry* paid a 'show the flag' visit to the Pool of London between 6th and 10th October 1965.

In 1966, the *Brighton* was retained as spare vessel and again carried out a series of Wednesday and Sunday excursions before finishing on 18th September after which she was offered for sale. Meanwhile the cargo vessels *Nantes* and *Rennes* were sold to Metaxas of Greece although the third of the trio, the *Brest*, was retained and closed the traditional cargo service during mid-February. Thereafter she was used on both the Folkestone – Boulogne and Weymouth – Channel Islands runs before following her sisters to the same Greek owners in October 1967.

During late 1964, the British Railways fleet had adopted the new identity and livery of British Rail. Gone were the

Top: The small ro-ro freighter **Capitaine Le Goff** *was acquired in 1972 but proved to be both slow and unstable and was disposed of just six years later. (John Hendy)*

Above: The 'V' class sisters are seen together at Dieppe. (Ferry Publicatiuons Library)

1 The Dieppe Years

black hulls and distinctive buff, black-topped funnels to be replaced by monastral blue hulls and red funnels with the BR double-arrow logo. Although the Newhaven – Dieppe fleet changed hull colours, to show that this was a two-thirds French service, the three remaining vessels retained their buff funnel colours until in December 1967, the *Valencay* returned from overhaul sporting the historic joint-service flag thus clearly stating the route's independence and separate identity.

With traffic continuing to grow, during autumn 1970, the British Railways Board ordered a new ship from the Brest Naval Dockyard. Initially known simply as 'CF3', she followed the design of the new Folkestone – Boulogne ferries *Hengist* and *Horsa* which were then building at the same yard. The *Falaise* was now just too small and had been earmarked to open a new car ferry service linking Weymouth and Jersey in 1973. Until the new ferry arrived on station, it became the norm to switch the Dover – Boulogne car ferry *Dover* to Newhaven each autumn to cover overhauls but for a couple of weeks in September-October 1971, the *Falaise* was surprisingly switched to operate between Dover and Calais. Meanwhile the Dieppe twins both saw a series of excursion charters with the *Villandry* visiting London in May 1970 after which she operated further trips to Jersey, Le Havre, Cherbourg and Rouen. Sadly these happy occasions were interspersed with irritating and unhappy labour problems, unrest and strikes which appeared to litter the following seasons and which finally culminated in the service's demise.

CONTINUED RO-RO GROWTH

During the early 1970s, roll on – roll off traffic was growing at an unprecedented rate which prompted SNCF to acquire a specialist freight vessel in the form of the *Capitaine Le Goff*. The vessel's selection was poor and did little to improve the overall situation on the Dieppe – Newhaven link. Her services were secured when she was bought off the stocks

In 1973 the **Senlac** *appeared from the Naval Dockyard at Brest and quickly proved to be a great asset to the Newhaven link. (FotoFlite)*

from Hatlo Verksted A/S of Ulsteinvik in Norway. Originally named *Admiral Carrier I*, the vessel was immediately renamed after Captain Jean Le Goff, Master of the cargo ship *Rennes* of 1925. During the Dunkirk evacuation, the steamer was ordered to Cherbourg to load explosives which would be used to dismantle the port installations once the evacuation was completed. Sadly the *Rennes* failed to reach Dunkirk and Le Goff and his ship were lost – the captain being seen as very much a local hero.

The vessel arrived at Dieppe on 27th July but berthing problems and manning arrangements prevented an early entry into service. Unfortunately the unpopular vessel proved both to be unstable and slow only managing a single round sailing each day. Following her final sailings in spring 1978 she was hastily sold to Saudi Arabian owners.

A visit at Newhaven by the new Folkestone car ferry *Hengist* en route to Dover from her builders at Brest on 7th June 1972, gave people in the Sussex town their first glimpse of the new breed of ferry and allayed local fears that the 'CF3' would not fit the port's linkspan.

A suitable name for the 'CF3' took some time to evolve. The British Railways Board were anxious to choose an English name associated with France. Eventually the name *Senlac* was selected, after the site of the Battle of Hastings in 1066. Other names suggested were 'Warrenne' (after Sir William of that name who was buried in the Cluniac priory at nearby Lewes), 'Verica' (an ancient King of Sussex) and even 'Seven Sisters' (after a line of nearby chalk cliffs).

Meanwhile the *Falaise* sailed to Holyhead in January 1973 where she was prepared for the final stage of an illustrious career. Sadly boiler problems now began to plague the ship and after she had failed for a final time in August 1974, she was towed to Bilbao for scrapping. Without doubt, history will see this small steamer as the vessel that saved the Newhaven – Dieppe link from closure and had later revitalised traffic to and from the Channel Islands.

The £4 million *Senlac* was officially named at a ceremony at Brest in March 1973 and duly arrived at Newhaven on 5th April. The ship boasted accommodation for 1,400 passengers and 210 cars (or 38 x 30ft lorries), double that of the vessel that she replaced. Although due in service with the 11.45 from Newhaven on 1st May, a strike saw her maiden departure put back by 24 hours. A further new passenger terminal was opened at the Sussex port that October.

The year-old Calais vessel *Chartres* was sent to relieve on the route during January 1975 while in sharp contrast the elderly steamer car ferry *Lord Warden* (1952) was required to deputise for a failed *Villandry* in June. Sister ship *Valencay* found employment on the Calais – Folkestone/ Dover links during November while the *Chartres* relieved the *Senlac* during the same month.

The mid-1970s saw a tremendous expansion in roll on – roll off freight crossing the English Channel and the nationalised railway fleets of England, Belgium and France (by now all trading as Sealink) were inadequately prepared to deal with the traffic. Money was always tight and as the shadow of a future Channel Tunnel was always present, they were reluctant to invest in new tonnage at a time when many of the low-headroomed stern loaders already in service were comparatively new. The sensible and cheaper alternative was to convert existing tonnage to drive-through operation whilst stripping out vehicle decks and providing greater height for lorries. In the case of some vessels, this required major surgery involving the raising of the passenger decks above.

DRIVE-THROUGH

Following work on the Calais-based ferry *Chantilly* during the winter of 1975-76 and two British steamships, the *Villandry* and *Valencay* were also earmarked for conversion. Approximately two-thirds of their after accommodation was

A strike at Dieppe in August 1980 saw all three vessels laid up at Newhaven – left to right **Senlac**, **Valencay** *and* **Villandry**. *The railway-owned tug* **Meeching** *lies on the West Quay (right). (John Hendy)*

raised by 56cm and with the extra headroom provided on their vehicle decks, they would be able to carry 20, rather than the previous ten, lorries. At the same time, the after docking bridges were removed while the adjacent observation lounges were extended in their place. The *Villandry* was first to depart to Le Havre during autumn 1976 followed a year later by her sister ship.

The *Villandry* returned to service in late March 1977 but French newspapers carried an alarming report suggesting that the route could be closed. BR admitted that it was certainly losing money but they were looking at ways of increasing traffic by evaluating the possibility of a new link to Le Havre.

During this period, in order to cover for reliefs and absences, the *Chantilly* appeared on the route as did the BR steamers *Earl Leofric* and *Caledonian Princess*. Stranraer's redundant ro-ro vessel *Ulidia*, Irish Ferries' *Dundalk* and Townsend Thoresen's *Free Enterprise II* also provided cover.

A rival passenger service from Brighton Marina to Dieppe commenced in April 1979 using Jetlink Ferries' Boeing jetfoil *Flying Princess*. The SNCF crews again showed their willingness to strike in protest at the new link, a situation that grew worse towards the close of the year when it was rumoured that the 'V' sisters might be withdrawn. The Newhaven route had lost £3 million during 1978 with Schiaffino's freight services to Shoreham and Dover most certainly serving to weaken its market position.

New Year's Day 1979 saw the creation of Sealink UK Ltd, a wholly owned subsidiary of the British Railways Board and in 1981 it was announced that they intended to withdraw from the Newhaven – Dieppe Joint Service at the end of that year. In the meantime the British looked for cuts in the service, especially on night sailings, and felt that with a 50 – 50 share agreement they might at last start making profits with the *Senlac*. A record number of passengers were carried

1 The Dieppe Years

*In order to cope with the growth of freight traffic using the route, the **Villandry** and **Valencay** were converted to drive-through operations in 1976 and 1977. Their after accommodation was raised by 56 cm. (Miles Cowsill)*

during 1981 but the route still managed to lose some £3.5 million.

Sadly during meetings in January 1982, Sealink UK Ltd and SNCF were unable to renegotiate the 1862 Joint Service Agreement and so the *Senlac* was to be sold. Strikes soon spread throughout the Sealink UK fleet but on 9th February, a breakthrough was finally made. The *Senlac* would be retained and partnered by the Calais-based *Chartres* while the *Villandry* would be sold and the *Valencay* downgraded to spare vessel. The French Government had promised SNCF financial backing to charter a larger Swedish ferry which would eventually replace the *Chartres*.

The arrival of the *Chartres* at Dieppe during May 1982 prompted an immediate dispute over manning levels and, until such time that matters were resolved, the *Senlac* sailed from Newhaven to Boulogne.

The redundant *Villandry* was busy on charter between Stranraer and Larne during the summer before being urgently called back to assist at Calais in August after a collision between the *Chantilly* and the new *Cote d'Azur*. She later became the stand-by vessel at Calais receiving the red SNCF funnel in December 1983 after Sealink UK Ltd had sold their one-third share in the vessel. Further charters took place between Holyhead and Dun Laoghaire and Heysham and

THE SeaFrance YEARS

Right: The **Cornouailles** was chartered from Brittany Ferries between 1984 and 1986. *(Miles Cowsill)*

Bottom left: The **Chartres** appeared on the Dieppe service in May 1982 and effectively replaced the **Villandry** and **Valencay.** *(Miles Cowsill)*

Right: The **Villandry** was purchased outright by SNCF in 1983 and saw charter service in the Irish Sea and at Calais before her sale in August 1984. *(Miles Cowsill)*

1 The Dieppe Years

Douglas (Isle of Man) before, in August 1984, the *Villandry* was eventually sold to Agapitos Brothers of Piraeus and renamed *Olympia*.

The need for a much larger ro-ro vessel was fulfilled by the charter of the spare Brittany Ferries vessel *Cornouailles* in January 1984. With capacity for 500 passengers and 205 cars or 40 trailers and 30 cars, her arrival on station saw the withdrawal of the *Valencay* even though she had been rostered to operate during that summer's peak season. However, strikes by the crews of the *Senlac* against the privatisation of Sealink UK Ltd saw the *Valencay* reactivated, running from Dieppe to Dover Western Docks at the end of May.

A further freighter was switched to Dieppe when in October 1984, the displaced Dunkirk ro-ro vessel *Transcontainer 1* was acquired in order to run a new service to Portsmouth. This eventually started in the following March but closed in October after which the ship was returned to Dunkirk.

At the close of the year, the *Valencay* was sold to Strintzis Line of Greece and renamed *Eptanisos*.

One of the first actions taken by the privatised Sealink British Ferries (now part of the Sea Containers Group) in October 1984 was to announce the British withdrawal from the Newhaven – Dieppe route as from the following March when the *Senlac* would be sold to SNCF. Chairman James Sherwood stated that as the *Senlac* was only able to make two round sailings each day (as opposed to the four of vessels based at Dover and Folkestone), this effectively meant that fares and retail and catering sales were half price. The French received subsidies from the State, regional and local levels whereas Sealink received no subsidies at all.

The *Senlac*'s final day under the Red Ensign proved to be an emotional 31st January 1985 after which the ship sailed to Le Havre for dry-docking. The summer of 1985 was the first peacetime summer since 1825 that a British vessel had not plied from the Sussex coast to Dieppe.

Alongside at Dieppe is the **Transcontainer 1** *which was briefly switched from Dunkirk in March 1985 to operate a short-lived seven-month service to Portsmouth. (Miles Cowsill)*

More French strikes greeted the *Senlac*'s return in full SNCF ownership during late February.

DIEPPE FERRIES

During late spring 1986, SNCF formed a subsidiary company, Dieppe Ferries, to manage the future of their Newhaven service. Mindful of the fact that the service's reliability rating was poor, passengers that had suffered from a cancelled sailing were now offered a free passage and a major campaign to attract new business was launched. The company stated that they wished both to enhance the quality of their service and upgrade their business. SNCF gave Dieppe Ferries four years to turn the loss-making route into profit.

Early in 1986, there were rumours that Dieppe Ferries were looking at the possibility of operating their service to Shoreham and plans for a new port at Dieppe were also revealed. Both Newhaven and Dieppe were Victorian ports and neither was geared up to handle the increasing volumes of freight or the larger vessels which the service so badly

required. The arrival of the 20-year-old Calais ferry *Chantilly* following a £600,000 refit in readiness for the 1986 season saw the *Cornouailles* returned to Brittany Ferries but she was hardly the ship that the route so desperately needed to turn around its ailing fortunes.

The refit took place at Le Havre and greatly changed the look and facilities offered by the vessel. Her forward bar area was extended by 12ft in which a small supermarket was fitted. This had the advantage of providing a roof which was adapted as a forward viewing platform for passengers. A lorry drivers' rest room was also created in addition to a new waiter service restaurant and a new general lounge with 350 reclining seats. As will be seen from the illustrations, her modified paintwork did little to enhance the ship's overall appearance.

A ro-ro vessel was now chartered for a two-year period from March 1986. Once again the choice of vessel showed the company management to be less than effective in their vessel selection; the Canadian *Marine Evangeline* (ex *Duke of Yorkshire*) was soon found to be difficult to load and a sub-charter was hastily sought.

However, more positive news was to hand following the two-year charter of the spare Stena Line vessel *Stena Nautica*, (ex *Stena Danica*, ex *Stena Nordica*) from April 1987. Built in Yugoslavia in 1974, the vessel's capacity was for as many as 1,800 passengers and 425 cars, almost double that of the *Chartres* and *Senlac*. Some £750,000 was immediately spent on her accommodation including a new Euro-Lounge, coffee shop and aircraft-style seating in addition to a new internal ramp.

At the end of the British involvement with the route in January 1985, the **Senlac** *was purchased outright by SNCF and is seen leaving Dieppe bathed in late afternoon light.* (Miles Cowsill)

1 The Dieppe Years

Top: The **Chantilly** replaced the chartered **Cornouailles** in 1986 but was in turn replaced by the **Versailles** in the following year. (Miles Cowsill)

Above: A two-year charter of the Canadian-owned freight ship **Marine Evangeline** in March 1986 proved something of a disaster and Dieppe Ferries quickly looked for a sub-charter. (Bernard McCall)

Right: On 25th January 1990, the **Chartres** arrived at Dieppe in a sinking condition after hitting the pier in storm conditions on arrival from Newhaven and sustaining a 45 metre gash below the waterline. She was temporarily replaced by the Belgian ferry **Prince Laurent**. (Ferry Publications Library)

Following a newspaper competition, the new vessel was named *Versailles* – 'a palace by name, a palace by nature' so ran the early advertisements. Extensive dredging was carried out at Newhaven so that the port could now accommodate vessels of up to 127 metres long with a 5.5-metre draft. The *Chartres* too was given an extensive £750,000 overhaul but in a bid to save losses on the route, the *Chantilly* was withdrawn and the *Senlac* offered for sale. The former passed to Agapitos Brothers as their *Olympia* whilst the latter enjoyed a summer charter on the Fishguard – Rosslare link. She was sold in late December to Ventouris Coast Lines of Greece for £1.7 million for whom she traded as the *Apollo Express I*.

The *Versailles* duly took up station on Easter Day (19th April) 1987 but engine troubles in August saw the transfer of the Dunkirk train ferry *Saint Eloi* which was followed from lay-up in the River Fal by the redundant *Vortigern*. Engine troubles in the new ship sadly continued and so the services of the Swedish-flagged *Gotland* (having recently finished a charter with Brittany Ferries) were hastily acquired.

A serious accident to the *Chartres* in January 1990 resulted in the flooding of her engine room and she limped off service for repairs in Rouen. At this time the spare Belgian ferry *Prince Laurent* was brought in but her rather basic interior and lack of facilities were the cause of many complaints. The *Chartres* did not return to Dieppe and her final three years were spent operating seasonal train-connected services between Calais and Dover Western Docks although some interesting winter diversions were also to come her way.

*"A palace by name and a palace by nature"- so ran the early publicity material relating to the **Versailles**. (Miles Cowsill).*

The **Chartres** in her element on a morning sailing to Dieppe with the Seven Sisters and Beachy Head to port. (FotoFlite)

THE SeaFrance YEARS

SEALINK SNAT

During early 1990, Sealink British Ferries was taken over by the Swedish company, Stena Line AB. Although their influence was not directly felt on the SNCF-controlled and operated Dieppe Ferries service, both Stena and SNCF were partners on the Dover Strait services and the arrival of the newly rebuilt *Fiesta* in June effectively released the *Champs Elysees* for the Dieppe link. The 1984-built ship underwent a three-month period of refurbishment at Dunkirk which included the fitting of a Euro-Lounge and reclining seats.

The summer of 1990 saw the *Versailles* and the *Champs Elysees* operating together in a new livery – that of Sealink SNAT (Societe Nouvelle d'Armement Transmanche) following a reorganisation of SNCF's ferry division and the split from the nationalised railway services in order to solve any conflict of interests following the opening of the Channel Tunnel. SNCF retained 90 per cent of a 51 per cent share in the ownership of the vessels with firstly Sealink British Ferries and then Sealink Stena Line holding the other 49 per cent. Sealink SNAT operated and managed the ships on their behalf and superseded Sealink Dieppe Ferries.

The *Champs Elysees* took up the link as from 2nd July and had accommodation for 1,800 passengers, 330 cars and 810 metres of freight. Following her hefty repairs, the *Chartres* was duly returned to Calais for the summer train-connected passenger services to Dover Western Docks, a service on which she was to operate until September 1993. She too passed to Agapitos for whom she was renamed *Express Santorini*.

To state that labour relations at Dieppe were sensitive is to grossly underestimate the situation which then existed. The service was strikebound for a complete month in June-July 1991 and although matters of this type are usually extremely complex and full of claim and counter-claim, they tended to centre on manning arrangements which the new SNAT management now insisted were rewritten. The seamen stated

1 The Dieppe Years

The **Champs Elysees** strikebound in Dieppe following the closure of the SNCF service in March 1992. (John Hendy)

The former **Versailles** became the **Stena Londoner** when she restarted the service in May 1992. (Miles Cowsill)

that changes in working conditions required 12 months' notice: the result was stalemate.

The route was still losing money and had gained the unenviable reputation for being the most unreliable ferry service in NW Europe. In the *Champs Elysees* and *Versailles* there was £6 million worth of investment sitting idle and during December 1991, one final ultimatum was issued: six months in which to resolve the problems or closure. This all culminated on 26th March 1992 when Sealink SNAT made their historic announcement that the service was to close at the end of April.

Anticipating this news four days earlier, the crews had gone on strike for a final time.

THE SeaFrance YEARS

Above, below and right: The **Stena Parisien** (*ex* **Champs Elysees**) *at Dieppe on the occasion of the opening of the port's new car ferry terminal in the outer harbour in July 1994. (Miles Cowsill/Stena Line)*

AFTER SEALINK SNAT

Although the history of the post-war SNCF involvement in the route effectively ends at this point, it is necessary to see the story through to its conclusion.

A number of potential bidders made offers for the loss-making service but the surprise buyers were Sealink Stena Line who restarted the service on 22nd May at just 28 hours' notice. This was a particularly odd move especially as the company were then involved in a serious cost-cutting exercise which had previously seen them axe the Folkestone – Boulogne link but had they not intervened then the Ramsgate operators Sally Line were in the wings ready to do so.

The *Versailles* had been strike-bound at Le Havre and had been moved from there to Southampton where she had been repainted in her new livery and been given a British crew. The ship was renamed *Stena Londoner* and left Newhaven at 10.00 that day to be met by thousands of townspeople as she entered Dieppe for the first time under her new ownership.

1 The Dieppe Years

With the *Champs Elysees* still blocking the linkspan, the 'Londoner' was forced to use the freight linkspan in the inner tidal harbour but now realising that the game was up, four days later the surviving strikers walked off the *Champs Elysees*. She was also sent to Southampton and was renamed *Stena Parisien*, retaining her Dieppe port of registry and with a French crew employed on a no strike agreement: the ship duly re-entered service on 3rd June.

For a while things looked bright with over a million passengers being carried by mid-October 1993. An extra freight ship, the Italian vessel *Vinzia E* (ex *Norcrest*) was taken on a two-year charter, confidence returned and with some aggressive marketing and fare reductions the route began its long return to profitability.

The new port at Dieppe was duly opened in July 1994 speeding up both crossing and turn round times and easing traffic congestion in and around the historic centre of Dieppe.

During the New Year 1993, the *Stena Londoner* operated in a freight capacity on the Southampton – Cherbourg link, her lack of cabins making her unsuitable for passenger use on the longer crossing.

The fast craft *Stena Sea Lynx II* made an appearance at Newhaven in February 1995 with much media-hype and expectation for the coming season. Meanwhile the names of the *Stena Antrim* (ex *St Christopher*) and *Stena Cambria* (ex *St Anselm*) were being suggested as long-term replacements for the 'Londoner' and 'Parisien' although traffic was significantly down during 1995 at a time of increased competition in the Western Channel.

The removal of the *Stena Londoner* and *Stena Parisien* from the Dieppe route was somewhat forced by the formation of

Ready for her new operators - the **Stena Parisien** *was formly the* **Champs Elysees**. *(Miles Cowsill)*

The **Stena Parisien** arriving at Newhaven shortly before being handed back to SNCF/SeaFrance in February 1997. (John Hendy)

Taking up service in July 1996, the fast craft **Stena Pegasus** proved to be an operational failure and her lack of reliability seriously affected the route's popularity. (Miles Cowsill)

The **Stena Lynx** was a 74 metre InCat craft which briefly served the route between April and July 1996. (John Bryant)

1 The Dieppe Years

The **Stena Antrim** (ex **St Christopher** of the Dover-Calais service) served out her final days on the Dieppe route until her sale in 1998. (John Bryant)

SeaFrance in 1996. Thereafter Stena Line seemed to lose direction, particularly as far as providing suitable and stable vessel selection was concerned.

As we shall see later, the joint-service between Stena and Sealink SNAT had been terminated by the French on the final day of 1995 and they were in need of ships with which to operate their new link. The 'Londoner' was returned to SeaFrance at Calais in April 1996 and renamed *SeaFrance Monet* after which her place at Dieppe was due to be taken by the new *Stena Lynx IV* which carried 148 cars and 600 passengers. With a top speed of 37 knots, the craft was expected to cut the crossing time to just two hours but was unfortunately arrested on passage to Britain from Tasmania. In the event the smaller 74-metre *Stena Lynx I* took up station in April with the unsuitable freighter *Marine Evangeline* picking up the lorry traffic. Then in July the Italian monohull *Stena Pegasus* took up the fast ferry crossing. Although on paper a better option than the InCat craft with a 50 per cent greater capacity, the vessel proved to be something of a disaster. Due to her poor operational performance, both reliability and sea-keeping, sailings were cancelled and traffic was lost so that in October 1996 she was hastily replaced by the *Stena Antrim* which had been superseded at Stranraer.

A Joint Service Agreement between P&O European Ferries and Stena Line came into force on New Year's Day 1997 and involved operations at both Dover and Newhaven. Much re-evaluation was carried out and with P&O now the major partners in the venture, there was immediate concern over the Dieppe route's future as in order to fight the Channel Tunnel, P&O were anxious to strengthen their position on the Dover – Calais link and were cutting their secondary services.

The *Stena Parisien* was eventually handed back to SeaFrance in January 1997 and was renamed *SeaFrance Manet*. Her place at Dieppe was briefly taken by the *Stena Cambria* in February. The following month saw her replaced with the introduction of the fast craft *Stena Lynx III* from Dover and during the summer months she offered three daily crossings against the *Stena Antrim*'s two.

Trials at both ports were carried out by the *Pride of Bruges* but it was eventually decided to use the 'Cambria' (with her more modern passenger accommodation) in place of her sister the 'Antrim'. Meanwhile the 81-metre *Stena Lynx III* was renamed *Elite* and during 1998 she operated the route on a

THE SeaFrance YEARS

three times a day basis. The *Stena Cambria* took up regular service (vice her sister) in April 1998 but it turned out to be a disastrous season with passenger numbers down 62 per cent and freight by 33 per cent. The *Elite* was proving to be so unreliable that she was withdrawn from service during October and amidst much acrimony, the historic link was finally closed on 31st January 1999. It was claimed that the service had lost £27 million since 1995.

The owners of Newhaven port, Sea Containers, would restart the service using a fast craft in April.

Although Transmanche Ferries use their small *Seven Sisters* on the Newhaven – Dieppe route today, the service struggles to make an impact. The failure of any investment at a very neglected port of Newhaven has been significant as has the poor port infrastructure which now leads through the South Downs National Park. With Dover to the east and Portsmouth to the west, Newhaven's future looks bleak.

The **Stena Lynx III** *became the* **Elite** *for the P&OStena Line joint venture but at the close of 1998 season she was quickly removed as being unreliable. (Miles Cowsill)*

The route's final former railway vessel was the **Stena Cambria** *(ex* **St Anselm***) which closed the link on 31st January 1999. (Miles Cowsill).*

CHAPTER 2

The Dunkirk Years

SEAFRANCE

THE SeaFrance YEARS

The route linking Dunkirk and Dover was established by the Southern Railway Company in October 1936, although it was not until 1951 that SNCF provided their first vessel for the service.

The three identical ships were provided by Swan Hunter & Wigham Richardson at Wallsend-on-Tyne and named after a trio of ferry crossing places on the River Thames which were served by the Southern. The Twickenham Ferry and Hampton Ferry were ready in 1934 while the Shepperton Ferry followed a year later. With it necessary to have the rails on board the ships and rails ashore both level, special berthing arrangements were required on both sides. At Dunkirk, the port was entered through a lock gate and the water level inside was constant but at Dover a special dock was constructed in order to achieve the correct rail alignment. Unfortunately the service was delayed while the Train Ferry Dock was lined with concrete in order to prevent water seeping out through fissures in the porous chalk on which the dock was built.

The 'Twickenham' was handed over to the Southern Railway's French subsidiary company, ALA (Angleterre Lorraine Alsace) as their traditional overnight service linking Folkestone and Dunkirk had ceased with the opening of the new service. This had commenced from Tilbury in 1927 (under the auspices of the London Midland & Scottish Railway) but was switched to the Southern's port three years later.

The Dunkirk train ferry carried mainly rail freight but each vessel was fitted with a garage at the after end of the Boat Deck which could accommodate some 25 cars which were driven on and off by means of fixed side ramps on both sides of the Channel. The odd lorry was also transported on the main train deck but this type of traffic was not encouraged as it was expected that all cross-Channel freight should be carried by train. The one exception to the usual

Top: Running astern into Dover's train ferry dock in 1972, the ALA steamer **Twickenham Ferry** was one of three sister ships built on the Tyne in 1934/35. (John Hendy)

Above: The **Saint-Germain**'s vestibule linked the bar/ saloon (forward) with the restaurant (aft). (John Hendy)

35

2 The Dunkirk Years

pattern of traffic occurred each evening with the arrival from London's Victoria and Paris' Gare du Nord of the fabled 'Night Ferry' Wagon-Lits sleeping cars which allowed passengers to arrive at their capital city of choice refreshed after a good night's sleep. That was the theory if not always the practice and in 1957, Brussels was also included as part of the service.

During the period of hostilities, the train ferries served as mine layers and as transports on the North Channel route between Stranraer and Larne and fortunately, all three survived to restart the service in December 1947.

The French had lost both of their pre-war passenger steamers during the Second World War and in 1951 introduced replacements. The *Cote d'Azur* (II) took up service on the Calais – Folkestone link while the train ferry *Saint-Germain* was built at the Helsingor Shipbuilding & Engineering Co in Denmark which was then the home of train ferry expertise.

Although of necessity, the same dimensions as the pre-war British ferries, the *Saint-Germain*'s fine lines and modern interior created a lasting impression which was to remain with her throughout her lengthy career. She was the first French ferry to be fitted with diesel engines (by Burmeister & Wain) and the application of her paintwork very much followed the design seen on many internal Danish ferries of the period. The prominent 'step-down' in hull colour below the bridge became the norm for all SNCF ferries for over 20 years and was also adopted by British Railways for their train ferries and for the 'Golden Arrow' steamer *Invicta* on which it looked dreadful.

The *Saint-Germain* arrived at Dunkirk from the builders on 24th July 1951 and entered service four days later. SNCF were delighted with their latest acquisition and planned more such vessels although there were the inevitable grumblings that she should have been built in France.

The **Saint-Germain** is seen leaving Dover when new in 1951. (FotoFlite)

2 The Dunkirk Years

*Leaving the new port of Dunkirk West in May 1986, the **Saint-Germain** vacates the train ferry berth for the incoming **Speedlink Vanguard** from Harwich. (John Hendy)*

Capacity was for 850 passengers with either 40 goods wagons or 12 sleeping cars on the two centre tracks from where passengers could alight onto platforms which allowed them to access the rest of the ship.

SNCF's first car ferry for the Dover – Calais route was scheduled to enter service on 30th May 1958. The *Compiegne* (of which more later) was built at Rouen but was delayed at the shipyard necessitating a replacement to maintain the link until the errant ferry finally arrived. Thus the *Saint-Germain* duly undertook trials at Dover's Eastern Docks in late April before taking up the car ferry roster until the *Compiegne* started service in late June. In this mode the 'Germain' could carry 135 cars on her train deck although there was no vehicle access to the boat deck garage.

During the latter 1950s and early 1960s, train ferries on the car ferry services to Calais and Boulogne became fairly

*The **Saint-Germain**'s comfortable forward bar/saloon very much reflected her Danish pedigree. (John Hendy)*

common summer occurrences until the arrival of the *Dover* in 1965. However, even then a period of mechanical trouble or an unexpected period of service would frequently see the 'Germain' back at work on the shorter routes. During August 1962 she was even briefly chartered to Townsend Bros Car Ferries after their new *Free Enterprise* had limped off service with bow rudder problems.

Roll on – roll off freight was accepted in 1959 and 34 large Whitbread tankers, each carrying 3,000 gallons, were shipped each week taking British beer to the Continent.

A joint train ferry service from Harwich to Dunkirk was opened by British Rail and SNCF in early October 1967. Operated by the *Norfolk Ferry*, the 'Germain' was called in to deputise at the end of the first month but the service was never very popular and soon closed.

The *Hampton Ferry* was the first of the original train ferries to depart when she was replaced at Dover by the new *Vortigern* in November 1969. The 'Shepperton' followed in September 1972 while the 'Twickenham' soldiered on until replaced by the new *Saint Eloi* in May 1974.

February 1974 had seen the entry into service of the multi-purpose (train/ car/ passenger) vessel *Chartres* which frequently worked the Dunkirk route when not required on the Calais station. Although transferred to the longer Dieppe – Newhaven route in May 1982, she returned to the Dunkirk – Dover train ferry run to operate reliefs in the winters of 1986 and 1987. As with BR's *Vortigern*, the *Chartres* was built to fit the confines of the old Train Ferry Dock and incorporated similar drive-on after garages accessed by fixed shore-based side linkspans. With their use as ro-ro freight carriers becoming more intense, their appearances as stern-loading train ferries eventually became spasmodic.

The greatest change to the service came in July 1976 when a new French terminal was opened up at Port Rapide near Gravelines. The Dunkirk West facility considerably

Top: The **Transcontainer 1** *moving up to the train ferry berth at Dover in July 1986. (John Hendy)*

Above: The 'TC1' *at the ro-ro berth at Dunkirk West in May 1986. (John Hendy)*

In 1976, the **Saint-Germain** received an extra 150-seater lounge on top of her after garage. (FotoFlite)

THE SeaFrance YEARS

improved crossing times, saving up to 70 minutes on the 33-mile passage to Dover. In anticipation of a growth in traffic, the *Saint-Germain* was fitted with a new 150-seat lounge on top of her after garage during 1976 but traffic continued to decline; the 'Night Ferry' service finished at the end of October 1980 with BR and SNCF unwilling to invest in new steel-bodied sleeping cars. The ship eventually became freight only from 20th February 1985 with her running partner, the *Saint Eloi* following suit in September that year.

Following the closure of the Harwich – Zeebrugge train ferry link, January 1987 saw the arrival of the *Cambridge Ferry* which assisted on the route for nearly two years.

SNCF's *Transcontainer 1* was built at La Seyne in 1968 but did not enter service on the Dunkirk – Harwich link until the following March. In 1974 she had rails added to her vehicle deck for service between Dunkirk and Dover/ Harwich in which role she could carry 36 wagons while at the end of the year she briefly carried freight between Calais and Dover.

The ALA train ferry **Saint Eloi** joined the Dunkirk-Dover link in 1974. (FotoFlite)

*The final ship to be built at Dunkirk was the **Nord Pas-de-Calais** which entered service on the train ferry link on 9th May 1988. The original design, by Hart Fenton for Sea Containers, was later adapted for SNCF's own use. (Miles Cowsill)*

Her name indicates that SNCF saw at least a second such ship in the series but she was never particularly successful and led rather a peripatetic career on a number of routes. In January 1975 she inaugurated a new thrice-weekly route between the recently opened Dunkirk West and Felixstowe which lasted until April 1984 after which she was transferred to Dieppe to operate the new Portsmouth route between March and October 1985. Her final service was again between Dunkirk West and Dover between February and July 1986 after which she was sold to a Greek company and spent the rest of her career in the eastern Mediterranean. She finished in operation across the Adriatic to Albania before being broken up in India during 2000.

The final ship ever to be built at the Normed yard at Dunkirk was the twin-decked train ferry *Nord Pas-de-Calais* which was a replacement for both smaller ships. She carried ro-ro freight on her upper deck while the lower deck was originally intended for rail freight. In order to accommodate

her, a huge new train ferry berth and associated linkspan were constructed at number 5 berth on Dover's Admiralty Pier but the hurricane force winds which occurred during the night of the Great Storm in October 1987 caused so much damage that the new ship was instead placed on Dover – Calais freight runs in December 1987 until such time that the new shore facilities were repaired. The 'NPC' finally took up train ferry service on 9th May 1988 with the 'Germain' carrying her final trains to the original Train Ferry Dock on the previous day. The ship was retained in service for a final week to carry ro-ro freight after which she was retired from service before sailing to India for demolition in August.

The Nord Pas-de-Calais' service speed of 22.5 knots allowed her to operate four times daily and it was anticipated that not only would her capacity match the combined capacity of the older two ships but also that of the recently withdrawn Harwich – Zeebrugge train ferry service.

On the lower of the two freight decks, six railway lines could accommodate 600 metres of rail freight plus a further 690 lane metres for ro-ro freight. The upper deck was designed to accommodate road freight only and could fit 710 lane metres. The 24 retractable buffers on the ship's train deck allowed the area to be used for ro-ro traffic at any time. A new double decker linkspan was also constructed adjacent to the original structure on the Quai d'Alsace at Dunkirk West.

The Channel Tunnel duly opened for business in May 1994 but the Nord Pas-de-Calais was retained in service primarily to carry the dangerous cargoes that the tunnel could not accommodate. In this role she carried about a million tons of Railfreight Distribution cargo each year although with more of this being directed at the tunnel, the route was finally axed on 22nd December 1995 after which time the 'NPC' was sent to work on the new SeaFrance service between Calais and Dover.

Top: The 'NPC' on passage to Dover and as she first appeared in 1988. *(Miles Cowsill)*

Above: The 'NPC' and her later modified Sealink SPN livery. *(John Hendy)*

CHAPTER 3
The Calais Years

As previously seen, both French pre-war passenger steamers were lost during hostilities. The *Cote d'Azur* (I) joined the Dover service in 1930 to be followed two years later by her sister ship *Cote d'Argent*. Remembering that the French railway system was not nationalised until 1938, their owners were SAGA (Societe Anonyme de Gerance et d'Armement). Accommodation was for 900 First Class and 500 Second Class passengers but both saw tragically short careers. The *Cote d'Azur* was lost during the Dunkirk evacuation on 27th May 1940 while her sister was later captured during the evacuation of La Pallice. Both were recycled by the German Navy and converted to minelayers before being lost in the western Baltic in April 1945 and June 1944.

In 1934 SAGA had attempted to sell its two turbine steamers to the Southern Railway Company but were prevented from doing so following the intervention of the Minister of Maritime Affairs who vetoed the sale. However, an agreement was reached with the Nord Railway to keep the ships under French control via a series of annual increments which were due to cease in 1950 after which time they would be fully railway owned. As we have seen, the railways of France were nationalised in 1938 and so this agreement duly passed to SNCF and their shipping division, the Armement Naval.

TWO NEW SHIPS

On 10th March 1948 SNCF's directors agreed to compensate SAGA for their share of loss of the twin pre-war steamers in order for the nationalised railway company to become ship owners in their own right.

The turbine steamer **Cote d'Azur** *(II) is seen going astern at Calais on her afternoon arrival from Folkestone. (Nigel Thornton collection)*

A remarkable photograph illustrating the surge of power generated by the **Cote d'Azur**'s *turbines as she prepares to go astern into Folkestone in June 1964. (FotoFlite)*

THE SeaFrance YEARS

In addition to the train ferry *Saint-Germain*, SNCF also introduced the fast turbine steamer *Cote d'Azur* (II) for the Calais – Folkestone service. Whereas the pre-war steamers were very much the French version of the Southern Railway's 'Golden Arrow' steamer *Canterbury*, when compared to her rather restrained post-war British counterparts, the second *Cote d'Azur* was a magnificent vessel with a thoroughly modern streamlined superstructure (much of which was aluminium) and funnel. The flair of her bows combined with a graceful sheer certainly created the impression of a flier although on the 90 minute short-sea route on which she was almost exclusively employed, her performance was always that of a greyhound on a leash.

The order was placed in January 1949 and the *Cote d'Azur* was built at an amazingly high cost of £1.4 million by Forges et Chantiers de la Mediterranee at Le Havre. Her launch on 3rd April 1950 was followed by a prolonged period of fitting out, before on her official trials off Cherbourg at the end of July in the following year, she attained a speed of 25.5 knots, her two sets of Parsons SR geared turbines generating some 22,000 shp and making her the most powerful cross-Channel steamer of her day. Needless to say, speeds of this nature were rarely seen in normal service which she commenced on 15th August. Managed by SAGA, as a result of which her funnel was white with a black top, within a year of entering service she had adopted the buff funnel of her owners. Interestingly, newspaper reports of the period indicate that SNCF intended to switch the Newhaven – Dieppe steamer *Lisieux* – in every way a smaller version of the *Cote d'Azur* – to operate the Calais – Folkestone service during her annual overhaul period but nothing appears to have come of this and British Railways' seasonal Folkestone – Boulogne vessels, *Isle of Thanet*, *Canterbury* or *Maid of Orleans* were drafted in instead.

On 5th October 1952, the legendary 'Golden Arrow'

3 The Calais Years

London – Paris through train, was diverted on its outward journey via Folkestone – Calais although the inward service continued through Dover. With the train departing from London Victoria at 13.00, the *Cote d'Azur* left Folkestone Harbour at 15.20 and arrived at Calais Maritime at 16.50. The reason behind this winter timetable diversion was to enable SNCF to use just one train and thereby make considerable financial savings. This arrangement lasted until May 1960 when the service was once more re-routed via Dover in both directions.

During late 1955, it was announced that an order for a new car and train ferry was about to be made from the Helsingor shipyard that had previously provided the *Saint-Germain* for the Dunkirk – Dover route. Nothing came of this but SNCF were much criticised by the French unions for having the train ferry built outside France. Interestingly, a report during late 1953 suggested that French steel was then 55 per cent higher in price than that made in the UK and that the French shipbuilding industry suffered from long delays in delivery while the distance of the yards from their sources of supply inevitably meant that French shipbuilding costs were 40 per cent higher.

Towards the end of the *Cote d'Azur*'s career, occasional early morning visits to Dover were made during the high season when she operated to Calais prior to her usual early afternoon sailing to Folkestone. With Folkestone being converted to a car ferry port in 1972, the *Cote d'Azur* completed her last sailing on 30th September prior to being replaced by the new multi-purpose vessel *Chartres* in 1974. To fill the gap, during 1973, SNCF chartered the British Rail car ferry *Normannia*.

The 'Cote' was eventually sold to new owners in Monaco and renamed *Marie F* for service to Sardinia although the scheme sadly fell through and the vessel was scrapped in Murcia, Spain, during 1974.

The premier French car ferry **Compiegne** joined the Calais – Dover route in June 1958 and is seen approaching Dover in June 1963. In February 1964, she trialled Newhaven's new car ferry berth although the linkspan was not then complete. (FotoFlite)

3 The Calais Years

Top: Townsend's **Free Enterprise** (left) and SNCF's **Compiegne** together maintained the Calais link from 1962 until 1965. (John Hendy)

Above: The **Compiegne** when new in 1958 dwarfs British Railway's double funnelled car ferry **Dinard** in her final season on the Boulogne route. (FotoFlite)

A FRENCH CAR FERRY

During the 1950s, British Railways operated the car ferries *Dinard* and *Lord Warden* on their Dover – Boulogne route while Townsend's converted frigate *Halladale* operated to Calais. These were very much seasonal operations for tourist cars at a time when winter traffic flows were minimal, there then being no freight shipped by car ferries.

SNCF's first contribution to the expanding car ferry fleets came in the form of the innovative *Compiegne*, the first such vessel to be built in France. As was then the tradition, all Calais-based ships were given names beginning with the letter 'C' and, with a garage on three decks for 164 cars, the new ferry would increase by more than 50 per cent of the number of spaces available on the railway-owned car ferries during the summer peak season. Passenger accommodation was for 1,000.

The ultra-modern vessel was built by Societe des Chantiers Reunis Loire-Normandie at the Grand Quevilly yard at Rouen. Launched on 7th March and expected in service on 30th May 1958, the *Compiegne* was billed as "the most modern and commodious car ferry on the cross-Channel short-sea services". She was in every respect a trend-setter with controllable pitch propellers operated from the bridge, a 125 hp bow thrust unit to help push her onto or away from her berths, of welded construction and also fitted with an after bridge to assist berthing at Dover and Calais. She was furnished in a very modern style and with fabrics designed to give the impression of light and space although her interior was rather more functional than luxurious. Her forward Boat Deck observation lounge was a special feature as was her snack bar with its daylight ceiling. On the Promenade Deck there was a large lounge and bar plus a restaurant for 132 people.

Two V16 Pielstick supercharged diesels, each of 4,500 hp and working at 345 rpm provided a service speed of 20

THE SeaFrance YEARS

Top left: The **Compiegne**'s garage accommodated 164 cars on three levels. (Nigel Thornton collection)

Above: Viewed from her after bridge, the **Compiegne**'s after decks provided popular all round views of the Channel. (Nigel Thornton collection)

Left: Coming astern into berth 1 at Dover Eastern Docks in August 1967, the **Compiegne** is captured at the moment her engines have been put 'Full Ahead' in order to slow her momentum. (John Hendy)

3 The Calais Years

On board the Compiegne

Top left: **Compiegne**: Dining Saloon.

Bottom left: **Compiegne**: Snack Bar.

Bottom right: **Compiegne**: Promenade Lounge.

(All Nigel Thornton collection)

Top left: **Compiegne**: Promenade Deck bar.

Left: **Compiegne**: Observation Lounge.

Above: **Compiegne**: driving off at Calais – note the limited size of the stern door.

(All Nigel Thornton collection)

The **Chantilly** was SNCF's second car ferry for the Calais station and entered service in June 1966. She is pictured after her conversion to drive-through operations in 1975-76. (FotoFlite)

THE SeaFrance YEARS

knots while the principal vehicle deck gave headroom of 12 feet 6 inches and the other two decks had headroom for 7 feet 4.5 inches. Ventilation of the car decks received special attention with exhaust gases being drawn off by suction pumps while fresh air was blown in.

Early in April 1958 it was announced that the new ship would be delayed by a month and so on the day of the grand opening of SNCF's new car ferry service, the train ferry *Saint-Germain* was called in to deputise. Eventually the *Compiegne* appeared and after running an inaugural cruise on 27th June, finally entered service on the following day, operating a single round sailing every 24 hours which was doubled up during summer season weekends. Her early schedule saw her leaving Calais at 10.15 and Dover at 13.30 while the extra weekend sailing left Calais at 17.00 and returned at 20.15.

Although the ship was warmly welcomed by the industry as a whole, a warning was given by Captain GD Walker, one of the senior Masters of the British Railways' fleet at Dover and Folkestone who was just about to retire as Master of the car ferry *Lord Warden*. Speaking at the annual dinner of the Marine Officers' Club in February 1958, Captain Walker spoke of the growing competition from the Belgians and French: "There is among the fleet grave and growing dismay and apprehension at what the years are likely to bring to our own jobs."

It was initially announced that as there was not sufficient traffic on the then secondary Calais route to keep the *Compiegne* in profit during the winter months, it was expected that she would assist on the BR Boulogne service at which time the receipts would be pooled. This occurred between October 1958 and the following January while on 28th October 1959, she took over the Folkestone services from the passenger steamer *Cote d'Azur* until the end of November. This latter substitution became the norm for a number of years although as she was only a one-class vessel, special areas

3 The Calais Years

Top: The **Chantilly** is seen leaving Dover when new in July 1966. (John Hendy)

Above: On board the **Chantilly**. (Nigel Thornton collection)

were reserved for the First Class 'Pullman' passengers on the outward 'Golden Arrow' runs.

So popular was the *Compiegne* that as early as August 1959, it was announced that consideration was being given to building a sister ship. As if to emphasise the requirement for a second ship on an expanding service, the train ferry *Saint-Germain* gave extra Calais car ferry sailings over three peak weekends during the 1960 peak season.

The success of the new SNCF ferry very much affected the rival Townsend service whose *Halladale* (55 cars, 388 passengers) was no real competition. Matters improved when in 1962, the *Free Enterprise* entered service although winter services were initially still shared between both companies.

With the drive-through ferry *Free Enterprise II* in service for Townsend in May 1965, SNCF's response was the £1.5 million *Chantilly* which was launched at Chantiers Dubigeon-Normandie, Nantes on 9th November that year. She was in every way an improved *Compiegne* and also an improvement on Dieppe's 'V' class sisters which had been introduced during 1965. With capacity for 210 cars and 1,200 passengers, the new ship introduced an escalator from the main vehicle deck directly into the passenger accommodation and also a special nursery for mothers with young children. The Promenade Deck boasted a 90-seater restaurant, a self-service cafeteria for 100 people, a saloon bar for 183 in addition to a small general lounge and ladies saloon each with 15 seats. The central section was fitted out with armchairs, settees and comfortable bench seating for 128, four double-berth cabins in addition to the shops, ticket and passport offices and also offices for the motoring organisations. On the Boat Deck, above, was a Panoramic forward saloon with 115 seats and a veranda bar and sun deck aft. A further innovation was the introduction of closed circuit television sets in the larger lounges.

Mechanically, the *Chantilly* was propelled by two 12-

cylinder Pielstick diesels each developing 4,750 hp at 370 rpm allowing the ship to cruise at 20.5 knots in service. Owing to the progress made in marine engineering since the introduction of the *Compiegne* eight years earlier, her 12-cylinder engines developed the same output as the earlier ship's 16-cylinder engines but both were particularly noisy vessels.

The *Chantilly* arrived in Calais as early as 1st June in readiness for an entry into service on 2nd July. Trials were carried out on the following day and a publicity trip took place five days later. There then followed visits to Boulogne, Newhaven and Dieppe on 8th June and a cruise from Dieppe to Rouen on 15th June. At this time cross-Channel trade was particularly problematical as the NUS had called a national seamen's strike and all BR and Townsend ships were laid up. The *Compiegne* soldiered on alone criss-crossing the Dover Strait with full loads and in need of an overhaul. It was therefore decided to place the *Chantilly* into traffic on 21st June vice the *Compiegne* although her 'official' entry into service on her own schedules commenced as planned on 2nd July. Unfortunately, a hawser around one of her propellers meant that two round sailings were missed.

At the end of her first season, the *Chantilly* was hastily chartered by Townsend Car Ferries for a period of one week from 29th October during which time they used her on the Zeebrugge route. This followed the grounding of the freighter *Autocarrier* off the Belgian port.

CALAIS BECOMES THE PREMIER PORT

The industry had effectively turned itself upside down when in 1970, British Rail (who until then had concentrated all car ferry services on their Boulogne route) opted instead to switch the main thrust of their operations to Calais. Between mid-July and mid-September some 64 weekly round Calais sailings would be offered instead of the 38 in

Top: Towards the end of her career in the Dover Strait, the passenger steamer **Cote d'Azur** *made early morning seasonal weekend visits to Dover. (Miles Cowsill)*

Above: A French failure was the introduction of the N500 'naviplane' **Ingenieur Jean Bertin** *which, after a number of modifications, was withdrawn in 1983. She is seen entering Dover Harbour in August 1978. (John Hendy)*

Creeping up to her linkspan at Calais, the **Chantilly** lifts her bow visor to reveal her watertight door beyond. (Miles Cowsill)

1969 while the Boulogne crossings were cut from 78 to 66 in the same period. The reason for this dramatic change in policy lay at the door of the British Rail hovercraft division, Seaspeed who had introduced twin SRN-4 craft onto the Dover – Boulogne route in June 1968 and August 1969. During the next ten years this ferry/ hovercraft competition was to rule the minds and planning of those who operated the service. Without doubt the ferry division suffered at a time when arch rivals Townsend Car Ferries were investing heavily in new ships and in a highly successful route to Belgium. Instead of competing with Townsend, British Rail, through its twin ferry and hovercraft subsidiaries, was effectively competing with itself.

The running down of the Dover – Boulogne route saw the older and smaller vessels placed on the route and thus the *Compiegne* and *Chantilly* became regulars on what was rapidly becoming the secondary crossing.

February 1972 had seen the *Chantilly* engaged in the import of Chrysler cars on the Dieppe – Newhaven route and the *Compiegne* was even tried until after two runs it was realised that she was not manoeuvrable enough within the confines of the French port. When in November 1975, the *Chartres* was sent to deputise at Dieppe in place of the *Valencay* which relieved the *Compiegne* for a month on the Calais – Dover/ Folkestone links.

A third new SNCF ferry was launched at Nantes on 12th September 1973. The original plan for the *Chartres* was to employ her on the Dover – Dunkirk train ferry link for nine months every year and during the peak summer period switch her to carry passengers, cars and freight between Calais and Folkestone. As she was a multi-purpose vessel, her hull size was based on the limitations imposed by Dover's Train Ferry Dock and in this respect she was similar to contemporary vessels BR's *Vortigern* and ALA's *Saint Eloi*.

The new ship proved to be an excellent addition to the

Two views of the **Chartres** arriving at Folkestone from Calais in August 1974. The ship was the most versatile of vessels being capable of carrying passengers, vehicles and trains on the Dunkirk-Dover service. (both John Hendy)

The **Chartres** as she appeared later in her career with SNCF funnel markings. (FotoFlite)

THE SeaFrance YEARS

fleet. Whilst there were similarities in the layout of her accommodation, like all train ferries there was an after garage which was accessed by side ramps at both Dover and Dunkirk. As with the 1969-built *Vortigern* (Britain's last train ferry) this area was later converted into a passenger lounge thereby reflecting her preferred use as a passenger/ car ferry. She was the first SNCF drive-through vessel to be built although only used her stern when operating as a train ferry. Capacity was for 240 cars or 22 freight vehicles in addition to 1,400 passengers. With freight capacity barely able to meet the burgeoning demand, drive-through ferries allowed easy access to the vehicle decks without the need to reverse lorries on board. The *Chantilly* was duly sent to Le Havre for conversion to drive-through operations between December 1975 and March 1976 and British Rail also converted their turbine car ferries *Holyhead Ferry I* and *Dover* which were renamed *Earl Leofric* and *Earl Siward*. At Dieppe the *Villandry* and *Valencay* were also converted while due to the nature of her construction, it was not possible to similarly treat the *Compiegne*. However, between October 1969 and January 1970, she was sent to Le Havre for her after section to be raised by 50cm in order to increase her limited freight capacity.

The one aspect of the *Chartres* which perhaps raised more comment than any other, was her enormous funnel. Ever since the advent of diesel-propelled vessels in the English Channel in 1934, small funnels had become the norm, it being perceived that the old-fashioned tall funnels associated with so many of the early turbine steamers were both outdated and unnecessary. However, the *Chartres* became the exception to the rule although there were suggestions from some that the shipyard had in fact placed it on the ship the wrong way round! The *Chartres* was blessed with ample outside deck space and became a most successful addition to the SNCF fleet.

61

3 The Calais Years

Top: The **Chantilly** leaving Dover-Western Docks on a train connected service to Calais during September 1985. (John Hendy)

Above: The **Compiegne** manoeuvring in the entrance of Dover Harbour in July 1977 before going astern to operate a mid-morning sailing to Boulogne. (John Hendy)

On her upper passenger deck (Deck B) the vessel's Panoramic Lounge and bar were very much as seen in the Compiegne and Chantilly. Aft of this were the waiter service restaurant 'Ile de France' while astern was the self-service cafeteria and a small discotheque. On the Promenade Deck (Deck C) below, the forward salon and bar were followed by wide promenades either side of the ship's offices and shops which led to the after saloon which was converted into the upper garage when the ship was serving as a train ferry.

The Chartres was a direct replacement for the passenger steamer Cote d'Azur (II) which had completed service in September 1972. To fill the gap between the departure of one vessel and the arrival of the second, SNCF purchased BR's Normannia for the 1973 (April – September) season during which time the ship was registered in Calais and operated with a French crew to both Calais and Boulogne.

After fitting out and trials, the Chartres arrived at Calais on 9th January 1974 and finally entered service in a freight mode between Dunkirk and Dover on 25th February. A brief break from this routine was given on 1st March when she performed her first passenger sailing with a 'special' between Dover and Calais when she carried English rugby supporters on their way to an international match in Paris. The vessel commenced regular passenger sailings on 28th May running from Calais and Boulogne to Dover while the winter timetable saw her back on the Dunkirk link.

At the beginning and end of 1975, the Chartres was on the Dieppe – Newhaven service and with the imminent arrival of the new Cote d'Azur (III) in 1981, it was originally planned to switch her permanently to the train ferry service in place of the 1951 Saint-Germain. As matters turned out, the 'Germain' was retained and the Chartres was instead transferred to the Dieppe station where she remained until 1990 with brief reappearances back on the train ferry link late in 1986 and 1988.

The opening of the new port at Dunkirk West in July 1976 saw BR's *Normannia* followed in November by the *Compiegne* attempting to start a roll on – roll off service in addition to the established train ferry link. The French ship was again sent to Dieppe in September 1977 after the *Valencay* had damaged herself. The summer season of 1979 saw both the *Compiegne* and *Chantilly* on the Dover – Boulogne route but with the advent of the new *Cote d'Azur* (III) neither would be required.

FLAGSHIP SERVICE

The early 1980s witnessed an unprecedented period of rivalry on the Dover – Calais service when the joint fleets of British Rail's Sealink UK Ltd and SNCF Armement Naval took on that of Townsend Thoresen. Each of the rival concerns provided three ships, the British Rail (Sealink) twins *St Anselm* (1980) and *St Christopher* (1981) being joined by the SNCF's new *Cote d'Azur* (III) in 1981. They were in competition with Townsend's three *Spirit of Free Enterprise* class ships but all six vessels represented a totally new phase and generation of cross-Channel ferry in so far as size and vehicle deck capacity was concerned. For the first time they were able to load and discharge on two decks simultaneously but whereas the Sealink UK ships were fitted with internal ramps linking the decks which could be used at other ports with only a single linkspan, the Townsend Thoresen trio's twin vehicle decks were quite separate with no connection between them. Reflecting their sub-60 minute pier-to-pier crossings, the Townsend operation was labelled the 'Blue Riband Service' whereas Sealink adopted the 'Flagship Service' for their own link. Much has been written concerning the performance of these vessels and the strengths and weaknesses of each design and it is not intended here to revisit the debate. Suffice to say that of the three Sealink vessels, the *Cote d'Azur* was clearly the pick of the bunch, not only in aesthetic terms but also in her

Top: The **Chartres** comes astern at Calais and passes the **Hengist** which is loading for Folkestone in May 1979. *(John Hendy)*

Above: During November 1986, the **Chartres** was returned from Dieppe to Dunkirk to operate the train ferry service during overhaul periods. *(John Hendy)*

The new **Cote d'Azur** (III) hurries towards Dover's western entrance on the occasion of her pre-service trials in September 1981. (FotoFlite)

THE SeaFrance YEARS

excellent passenger accommodation for 1,400 passengers. Her twin vehicle decks carried 330 cars or 43 pieces of freight.

The *Cote d'Azur* was built in the same yard at Le Havre as her two predecessors of that name by Ateliers et Chantiers du Havre and was launched on a rainy 22nd December 1980.

She carried almost twice the freight capacity of the previous generation of car ferries with five rows of freight on her main vehicle deck and three rows on her upper deck. A 40-tonne lift gave access to the upper deck should she ever be called to run from ports where there was only a single linkspan.

The ship's interior furnishing was carried out by Chantiers A. Baudet of Saint Nazaire based on the designs of Lionel Bureau of Nantes. Most internal reclining seats were SNCF coach design supplied by the Sofanor Company.

Her twin bow thrusters were each powered by 1,000 hp giving a lateral thrust of 12 tonnes while the two SEMT Pielstick engines each developed 11,250 hp. Through a reducing gear, their speed was reduced from 500 to 220 rpm.

Delays, which had blighted the entry into service of the two British Rail vessels, were now to cross the Channel and a mid-August delivery was put back by some six weeks as a result of which she missed the end of the summer season. As it was, the new ship finally arrived at Dover for trials on 28th September while on the following day she also carried out trials at Folkestone and Boulogne. Her maiden commercial voyage duly took place on 7th October although a strike delayed her official naming ceremony until 2nd December by which time she had replaced the *Chartres* in the local fleet. Until her arrival, the *Chartres* had been the French third of 'the Flagship service' although there was a period during January and February 1981 when the by now aged *Compiegne* had been raised from winter slumbers and called in to deputise.

3 The Calais Years

Top: In December 1981, the new **Cote d'Azur** was open to the public in the Pool of London. (John Hendy)

Above: The after Brasserie on Deck 8 of the **SeaFrance Renoir** (ex **Cote d'Azur**) (John Hendy)

Between 1st and 6th December the *Cote d'Azur* visited the Pool of London when she was moored alongside the preserved cruiser HMS *Belfast*. During this time the World Travel Market was being held at Olympia and the ship's vehicle decks were tastefully converted into showrooms publicising a variety of French goods.

WIND OF CHANGE

This period very much represented one of change in the local fleets with British Rail/ Sealink UK Ltd ridding themselves of their final earlier generation turbine steamers and SNCF also disposing of their older and smaller tonnage which was unable to carry satisfactory freight loadings.

After several periods of reactivation to assist during one crisis or another, the *Compiegne* was finally sold to Greek owners Strintzis and left Calais as the *Ionian Glory* on 24th October 1981. It had been calculated that during her 23-year career, the ship had completed 22,712 crossings of the English Channel. The former Newhaven vessel *Villandry* was on hand to effectively replace her as spare ship.

As for the *Chantilly*, she lingered on the seasonal Calais – Dover Western Docks train-connected services until replaced in 1984 by the new *Champs Elysees*. She finally finished local service in January 1985 after which she was transferred to the Dieppe station for the rest of her career with SNCF. However, her service was briefly terminated on 5th August 1982, when engaged on the 03.45 service to Calais, she was in collision off Calais with the new *Cote d'Azur* on the 02.00 to Dover. Both received considerable bow damage and the 'Cote' was immediately sent to Dunkirk where her damaged visor was removed and her watertight bow door sealed, running for the rest of the season as a stern loader. As for the *Chantilly*, with the ship so close to retirement, SNCF considered not repairing her, especially as the former Dieppe ferry *Villandry* was available for use in her place. However, the repairs were made and that November the ship even relieved on the 'Flagship Service' in place of the British flagged St Anselm.

Early in November 1982, an announcement was made concerning the closure of the Dover – Boulogne route which was by then simply operated as a seasonal service but which, ten years previously, had been the top link. A token Saturday afternoon link using the train ferry *Saint Eloi* was offered during the peak season of 1983 but it was hardly surprising that there were few takers.

BOULOGNE REVIVAL

During spring 1982, SNCF ordered a sister ship for the *Cote d'Azur* and went back to the Dubigeon Normandie yard at Nantes. It appears that the management of SNCF Armement Naval were not particularly anxious to receive a further ferry but the Mayor of Boulogne was set to improve the lot of the city he represented. A new £7 million double deck ramp was constructed at berth 13 and when opened in July 1984, it was stated that the new ship would have use of it. This prospect caused distinct problems for Sealink's route managers as the Boulogne service had long since ceased to play any significant role in the scheme of things and by putting the new ship on the route, this would simply serve to weaken their position on the now premier Calais service. The ship was duly named *Champs Elysees* and to indicate that she was not a Calais vessel, she was registered in Nantes.

Launched at Nantes on 21st December 1983, the *Champs Elysees* arrived at Calais on 30th September 1984 and the following day sailed to Boulogne for ramp tests. As she was a little late in arriving, she was hastily pressed into service and the maiden commercial voyage was the 07.30 from Calais to Dover on 4th October. With her capacity for 300 cars or 54 x 15-metre freight vehicles in addition to 1,800 passengers, she was the largest Sealink vessel in service across the Dover Strait.

*Top: A view from the starboard bridge wing of the **Champs Elysees** as she nears Calais on 7th October 1984. The rival **Herald of Free Enterprise** follows in her wake. (John Hendy)*

*Above: The **Champs Elysees** entering Dover Harbour when new on 7th October 1984. (John Hendy)*

3 The Calais Years

Contemporary press reports made much of her 'mammoth shopping arcade' selling a variety of duty-free goods and designed for maximum throughput throughout the 90-minute crossing. In addition to this, the ship also boasted a 300-seater self-service restaurant, a Buffet Express self-service restaurant for snacks and light refreshments which seated 200, two bars with lounge seating for 400, a nursery for mothers and young children in addition to facilities for handicapped travellers. Most importantly a lift was provided from the vehicle decks into the ship's accommodation. Lorry drivers also had their own private lounge and restaurant whilst throughout the ship, her excellent signage was both clear and concise. The ship's facilities were certainly an advance on the earlier *Cote d'Azur* (III) although with her slimmer funnel and more angular forward appearance, aesthetically her looks did not quite match those of her running partner.

The *Champs Elysees* was a most attractive vessel in which her designers had made the maximum use of light by fitting large panoramic windows and reflective surfaces. Muted colour schemes throughout made for a relaxing atmosphere and as with all SNCF vessels, their passengers would have immediately known that they were on board a French ship given that special ambience which the French have always been so good at achieving.

Boulogne sailings were revived on Wednesdays and Saturdays from 19th January 1985 with the *Champs Elysees* running the 09.30 and 15.30 from Dover until 20th March when the timings were modified to 10.15 and 16.30. However, with such an infrequent service it was always going to present a challenge and as from 1st July the Wednesday sailings were cancelled. From 28th September, the British ship *St David* slotted into the Saturday runs after being ousted from the Dover – Ostend link but, on her departure to the Irish Sea, the last rites were carried out by the *Cote d'Azur*

Registered in Nantes, the **Champs Elysees** approaches Dover on trials. (FotoFlite)

3 The Calais Years

Top: The **Cote d'Azur** leaving Calais astern.

Bottom left: The **Champs Elysees** arriving at Calais from the builders.

Bottom right: The **Champs Elysees** approaching Calais.

(All Miles Cowsill)

THE SeaFrance YEARS

SNCF adopted a livery change after operating partners Sealink UK Ltd had introduced a white hull in readiness for privatisation in 1984. The **Champs Elysees** nears Calais (top) while the **Cote d'Azur** (bottom) heads away from her home port en route to Dover. (both John Hendy)

3 The Calais Years

Top: The ALA train ferry **Saint Eloi** *was chartered to SNCF during the summer of 1988 in order to operate the train connected services from Dover West Docks to Calais Maritime. On 23rd July she had the misfortune to hit the quay at Dover which resulted in serious bow damage and she is seen arriving at Calais later in the day. (Miles Cowsill)*

Above: In the following year the ship was renamed **Channel Entente** *and came under British management. (Miles Cowsill)*

during the New Year.

The railway-owned Sealink UK Ltd was de-nationalised in July 1984 and now traded as Sealink British Ferries, its new owners being Sea Containers of Bermuda. For SNCF little was to change although Sea Containers soon managed to alienate their one time Belgian partners in the Sealink consortium by attempting to increase their 15 per cent to a 50 per cent share of the Ostend traffic. This effectively shut them out of both Ostend and Zeebrugge and resulted in the Belgians adopting new partners in their former rivals Townsend Thoresen.

The French twins received white hulls during their overhauls in the winter of 1987-88 at which time the *Champs Elysees* was re-registered in Calais.

In February 1988, with the new train ferry *Nord Pas-de-Calais* unable to commence service from Dunkirk to Dover due to storm damage at the train ferry berth on the Admiralty Pier, she took up freight sailings from Dover Eastern Docks to Calais until the berth was completed in early May. With the 'NPC' in service, the *Saint-Germain* was retired and the *Saint Eloi* found summer employment running the train-connected services between Calais Maritime and Dover Western Docks. Wholly owned by Sealink British Ferries' French subsidiary the Angleterre-Lorraine-Alsace SA de Navigation (ALA) she operated with an SNCF crew but this was an unhappy period of her career and she subsequently appeared in the following year named *Channel Entente* and adorned in the livery and crew of her owners.

With the *Channel Entente* sold to the Isle of Man Steam Packet Company, the *Chartres* was brought back from the Dieppe station to work the summer Calais – Dover Western Docks services in 1990 and continued to operate this service until her own withdrawal on 24th September 1993. She appeared with the ALA logo on her funnel as she was effectively on charter to the Sealink British Ferries subsidiary company.

SEALINK SNAT TAKE THE HELM

With the Channel Tunnel finally under construction, P&O European Ferries seized the proverbial bull by the horns and ordered the twin 'Chunnel Beaters' *Pride of Dover* and *Pride of Calais*. These largest yet ferries for the Dover Strait entered service in June and December 1987 and, in terms of facilities and vehicle deck space eclipsed all other ferries then in operation. The industry waited to see how their competitors in the Sealink consortium would respond and during 1986 there were plans to stretch both the previous generation ships *St Anselm* and *St Christopher* by either inserting a 50ft or 100ft section amidships.

At a time when SNCF were heavily involved both in the Channel Tunnel project and also TGV Nord, the French Government were pondering whether to rid themselves of their shipping division. Should the sale go ahead then Sea Containers was planning the acquisition of SNCF Armement Naval. During October 1987, Sea Containers certainly

*Following the departure of the **Channel Entente** for the Isle of Man in early 1990, the **Chartres** was called in to operate the summer train connected services between Dover Western Docks and Calais Maritime on charter to the British subsidiary, ALA. She is seen arriving at Calais that summer. She closed the service on 24th September 1993. (John Hendy).*

believed that the green light had been given from Paris and stated that if the deal went ahead then both the *Cote d'Azur* and *Champs Elysees* would be stretched along with their British counterparts. By November 1988, negotiations had continued and it was announced that Sealink British Ferries were "poised to take over the cross-Channel services of SNCF". An agreement had been reached in principle under which Sealink British Ferries would be given the first option to buy all five SNCF vessels in 1993 although approval was still awaited from the French Government. So far so good but when the French Transport Minister instructed SNCF to consult with the shipping unions the months of negotiations came to an abrupt halt with a resounding "Non!"

However, in autumn 1988 came the news that Sea Containers, the parent company of the privatised Sealink British Ferries, had acquired a pair of Bulgarian-owned deep-sea ro-ro 'Challenger' class ferries for conversion. One of

The **Champs Elysees** is seen crossing to Calais before her funnel markings were stylised. (FotoFlite)

THE SeaFrance YEARS

them, renamed *Channel Seaway*, operated mainly in a freight mode between Dover and Calais between May and October 1989 before joining her sister which was already at Lloyd Werft Bremerhaven undergoing her major conversion.

In order that both British and French partners in the Sealink pool should receive the equal benefit of a new ship, it was necessary to float a new joint venture company which effectively separated the pro-Channel Tunnel SNCF from its shipping division which obviously opposed it.

After 12 months of negotiations, during October 1989 plans were announced for a joint venture company to take over the ownership of SNCF vessels operating on the Calais – Dover and Dieppe – Newhaven services. Operating partners Sealink British Ferries were invited to acquire a 49 per cent interest in the new company.

A condition of the new structure was that the joint venture would purchase the *Fiesta* and also extensively refurbish the other three ships. The *Cote d'Azur* was allocated £2 million for her refurbishment while a total of £3 million would be spent on the *Champs Elysees* and *Versailles* at Dieppe.

SNCF and the capital investment company CGMF (Compagnie Generale Maritime et Financiere) were to be partners in a new group STM in which SNCF would hold a 90 per cent share.

This public sector group then took 51 per cent of the equity of SPN (Societe Propietaire des Navaires) who were to own the ships with the British Sealink partners taking the other 49 per cent.

The ships' operators were be to SNAT (Societe Nouvelle d'Armement Transmanche) in which STM held a 70 per cent share, the other 30 per cent being held by various regional and professional interests.

On the surface this appears to be a somewhat complex arrangement but simply put, it meant that SPN acquired the ships and chartered them to SNAT who were to partner

3 The Calais Years

Top: The freight vessel **Channel Seaway** *was operated by Sealink British Ferries during the 1989 season prior to being sent to Bremerhaven for conversion to the* **Fiesta**. *(Miles Cowsill)*

Above: Yet another livery change occurred when in 1990 ship ownership passed from SNCF Armement Naval to Sealink SPN. The **Cote d'Azur** *heads away from Calais in April that year. (John Hendy)*

Sealink British Ferries in the Sealink pool and take over Armement Naval's operating and commercial functions.

The new company came into being on 16th January 1989 and acquired the *Fiesta* six days later.

The newly converted ships represented two of a trio of deep-sea vessels which were built in 1979 by Kockums Varv (Shipyard) AB in Malmo, Sweden. Originally the *Zenobia*, *Scandinavia* and *Ariadne*, the lead ship of the trio was lost with £200 million worth of cargo off Larnaca, Cyprus during her maiden voyage in June 1980. The fault apparently lay in the failure of her computerised pumping system which pumped too much excess water into her ballast tanks.

The *Ariadne* was launched for Rederi AB Nordo of Malmo on 13th October 1979 and was renamed *Soca* before entering service in the following February. In 1981 she was sold to Bulgarian owners SOMAT and renamed *Trapezitza* for service with Medlink. During this period she was a regular visitor to Iran and Iraq before passing for further charters to Greek and then to Danish owners DFDS. In October 1988 she was purchased by Sealink and renamed *Fantasia* before becoming the *Channel Seaway* on 7th May the following year. At the end of her Dover season she was sent to Bremerhaven for conversion and arrived in the German yard on 17th October. In the yard the ships exchanged names so that the British ship (named *Fiesta*) took the name *Fantasia* while the original *Fantasia* became *Fiesta* – this at the request of the French management who were unhappy about the French translation of their originally allocated vessel.

The converted ship arrived in Calais on 13th May 1990 but manning problems prevented her from entering service in a freight mode until 1st July. The ship entered full passenger service eight days later allowing the *Champs Elysees* to switch to the Dieppe – Newhaven service.

The conversion of the *Fantasia* and *Fiesta* was extremely demanding and involved the addition of some 2,000 tonnes

of steel and the cutting-free and lowering by approximately 1.8 metres forward and 2.8 metres aft of the whole of the upper vehicle deck weighing some 900 tonnes. This allowed the construction of a completely new vehicle deck inside the existing superstructure while the addition of extensive sponsons along each side of the ship not only improved stability but also allowed her to remain upright in the event of hull penetration.

Added to all this, a new bow visor with inner watertight doors, new doors allowing vehicles to drive on/off at two levels, the replacement of all life-saving equipment (and the adoption of the RFD Marine Escape System), the fitting of an additional bow-thruster, the fitting of new Becker-type rudders and the complete redesign of both exterior and interior all demanded a high standard of design throughout.

The result was a pair of ships which looked like no others and in truth, they certainly looked as if they had been converted from something else as it was almost inconceivable that any naval architect would have created such profiles from scratch.

The interiors were designed by the American architect Warren Platner who set out to create a 'floating world' giving as much light and views of the sea as possible. Platner had previously designed the interiors for Sea Containers House on the River Thames' south bank and was awarded the ships' contract on the strength of both this and an outstanding reputation in the United States.

In order to achieve his 'floating world' the newly fitted windows were unusually large and almost every space was surrounded with glass on two or three sides. Even in areas of

The **Fiesta** *arriving at Calais when new in July 1990. Her arrival allowed the* **Champs Elysees** *to be transferred to Dieppe (John Hendy).*

3 The Calais Years

The **Fiesta** in service at Dover and towering above the P&OStena Line ferry **P&OSL Picardy**. (John Hendy)

low headroom, two-storey spaces and skylights were created along with unique decorative personalities for each facility on board. Signage was bold and eye-catching while the use of melamine plastics allowed a myriad of colours to decorate the ships. The forward two-tiered Motorists' Haven was certainly a 'first' and perhaps represented the most impressive area on board while the 'Speedy Gourmet', with its raised centre section, aimed to offer everyone the best seat in the house. Aft of this, passengers ascended into the Tax Free Shop while overlooking the generous open spaces of the after outside passenger deck was the Carnival Bar.

Platner's creation was unlike anything ever seen on the Dover – Calais route either previously or since and without doubt his striking interiors were responsible for a complete re-evaluation of interior ferry design. However, stunningly different as they were, many of the furnishings unfortunately failed to withstand the throughput of thousands of daily passengers and in this respect Platner's shore-based experience in designing luxury hotels put him at a disadvantage when providing his first interiors for the ferry industry. The British flag Fantasia was subsequently totally redesigned during the remaining course of her career although the Fiesta was not subjected to the same degree of modifications. Both ships were in Gothenburg during the early part of 1992 in order to improve their manoeuvrability when their original bow-thrust units were upgraded and an azimuth propeller was also fitted at their after ends.

For the Fiesta, a further refit took place at Le Havre early in 1994 when the new Galaxy Bar with full-length windows was fitted in the void-space below her sky dome. At the same time the Motorists' Lounge became the Globetrotter Café.

This was an unhappy time for Sealink SNAT with industrial unrest caused by the seemingly impossible tension on the Dieppe – Newhaven station. All services were suspended for a month from mid-June 1991 but once the link was finally axed in March 1992, the Calais station was left alone to determine its own future.

SEAFRANCE

During 1990, Sealink British Ferries and Sealink SNAT had signed a five-year extension to the longstanding pooling agreement on the Dover – Calais service. At this time SBF's parent company, Sea Containers, was in the process of fending off a hostile takeover bid which was finally lost in May 1990. The Swedish company Stena Line duly acquired the Sea Containers' ferry business (minus the Isle of Wight and hovercraft services) for £259 million and took over the operating and trading agreement with Sealink SNAT.

From the start, the French – Swedish relationship was constantly under strain and Stena's approach of "we know how to run ferries" and a rather more aggressive approach to business certainly failed to impress. Experienced senior

managers were dispensed with while the ships were fitted with American-style fast-food outlets and pumped out loud music throughout their interiors in an effort to attract a mass market as part of Stena's Travel Service Concept; Stena Vision was certainly not to everyone's taste. Needless to say it was expected that Stena's French partners (who still preferred to market themselves as Sealink) should follow suit; a cultural prospect which appeared somewhat alien to them. At the same time, the impending threat of the Channel Tunnel saw both Stena and rivals P&O (who had taken over Townsend Thoresen in December 1986) in talks concerning the possibility of an eventual joint service and there were French fears that they might possibly be excluded from any such arrangement.

M. Didier Bonnet (President of SNAT) duly announced, "After careful and exhaustive analysis of both companies' objectives and strategies, SNAT realised at the end of June 1995 that they were differing too widely and that it was not possible to come to a mutually satisfactory agreement." In July 1995 SNAT gave Stena notice that they intended to operate independently as from New Year's Day 1996 and would in future trade as SeaFrance. SNAT had previously held talks with P&O European Ferries concerning a joint service but these discussions had come to nothing.

During the New Year 1996, the *Fiesta* went off for annual refit and returned as the *SeaFrance Cezanne* complete with a new livery, re-branding and with all outlets on board now renamed in the new SeaFrance corporate style. Thus the Carnival Bar became Le Pub, the sky dome Galaxy Bar became the Café Parisien and La Brasserie was also created in the restaurant area.

Stena responded to the split by stating that they would bring their "full weight to bear in the key Continental tourist and freight short-sea sector to create an international service organisation capable of challenging any other operator." It

Top: The **SeaFrance Monet** alongside the former Gare Maritime at Calais. (John Hendy)

Above: The **SeaFrance Manet** arriving at Calais. Both ships had previously worked together on the Dieppe-Newhaven route. (John Hendy)

3 The Calais Years

wasn't long before their traffic figures showed them in third place behind P&O and SeaFrance.

SeaFrance planned to develop a specific Gallic identity and believed that this would be the key to developing their market share. During 1994, the Fiesta and Cote d'Azur had carried 15 per cent more passengers, 19 per cent more cars and 16 per cent more coaches and lorries than ever before. Financial results were excellent with a £154 million turnover and a £7.4 million profit before tax.

The Cote d'Azur's transformation to a SeaFrance ship saw her sail to Le Havre for a £5 million refit during January 1996 where she was substantially refurbished, particularly at the stern where her original after bridge was removed in favour of an upper area to an extended bar/ cafe. She reappeared as the SeaFrance Renoir and took up service during the following month. The Calais-based fleet was assisted by the ro-ro ferry SeaFrance Nord Pas-de-Calais which had finally closed the Dunkirk West train ferry link on 22nd December 1995 and which took up her new role on the following 7th January.

In order to improve their on-board catering, the company appointed a consultant chef to devise a series of monthly menus, reflecting seasonal ingredients, to be served in the ships' La Brasserie. This was in sharp contrast to Stena Line's McDonald's fast food outlets.

The major problem immediately faced by SeaFrance was a lack of ships with which to operate their new service. The Fiesta and Cote d'Azur had accompanied their Sealink fleet partners but extra ships were required in order to provide a balanced competition.

Help was at hand in the former Dieppe vessel Versailles which had been renamed Stena Londoner after Stena had taken over the Newhaven service in April 1992. As we have previously seen, after a bright start, matters started to lose their way and culminated in her withdrawal on 3rd March

During the early SeaFrance years, the **SeaFrance Monet** (ex **Versailles**) fulfilled a temporary role at Calais until replaced by the 'Manet'. Even then, she lingered on and operated winter reliefs. (FotoFlite)

3 The Calais Years

1996 after which she saw brief service at both Fishguard and Holyhead. With this work completed on 10th April this elderly vessel was sent for a £500,000 refit at Dunkirk and re-registered in France. Much of this work involved essential SOLAS modifications in order to keep the ship in class and in June she became the *SeaFrance Monet*, the seventh name in her 22-year career.

The ship took up service between Calais and Dover on 3rd July 1996 operating with the *SeaFrance Cezanne* and the former *Cote d'Azur* which had been renamed *SeaFrance Renoir*. The French were immediately accused of breaking international ferry safety rules, it being claimed that the ship had not qualified for one of her certificates and had only been given a temporary version of another. A spokesman for Bureau Veritas said that the vessel complied with French safety standards but a year's extension had been given to adopt new bow-door safety codes. However, the ship was never used on a year-round basis but simply to add to the summer schedules and to cover winter overhaul periods.

The *Versailles*' operating partner at Dieppe had been the *Champs Elysees* which Stena had renamed *Stena Parisien* for the commencement of her charter on 3rd June 1992. This was completed on 10th January 1997 after which she too was sent to Dunkirk for a £1 million overhaul during which time she became the *SeaFrance Manet*. Commencing service on 20th January, she effectively replaced the *SeaFrance Monet* in the fleet and it was then expected that the 'Monet' would be offered for sale as she was requiring hefty modifications to bring her up to new SOLAS standards. However, an emergency dry-docking for the 'Renoir' followed by mechanical problems with the 'Cezanne' saw the ship reactivated and used yet again during the refit periods in the following January.

SeaFrance had originally stated that their aim was to capture 12 per cent of the Dover – Calais cross-Channel market but some very aggressive undercutting of their

The **SeaFrance Renoir** (ex **Cote d'Azur**) arriving at Dover Eastern Docks as the freighter **SeaFrance Nord Pas-de-Calais** loads in berth 5. (John Hendy)

Top left: The **SeaFrance Cezanne** (ex **Fiesta**) is seen departing from Calais. (John Hendy)

Left: A busy scene at Dover in May 2008 as the **SeaFrance Renoir** arrives from Calais and allows the P&O ferry **Pride of Calais** to depart. (John Hendy)

Left: A powerful view of the **SeaFrance Manet** at speed in the Dover Strait. (FotoFlite)

The freighter **SeaFrance Nord Pas-de-Calais** is seen approaching Dover after having been made redundant as the Dunkirk train ferry. (FotoFlite)

competitors' rates saw 14.5 per cent of passengers and 20 per cent of the freight using the service within 18 months of its commencement.

A NEW GENERATION

Until this point in the SeaFrance story, in terms of the ships that they operated, the company very much lagged behind their British rivals on the Dover Strait. During the period of nationalised ownership of the British Rail/ Sealink UK Ltd fleets, investment in new tonnage was a constant problem. Not only were the limited funds available invariably directed at railway infrastructure but the ever-present threat of a Channel Tunnel was to blight the British railway fleet throughout its later history. Whereas, after an analysis of traffic trends, the independent Townsend Car Ferries could order a ship at a season's end and expect it in service for the following season, endless committees, re-evaluations and revised plans meant that it could take a year to decide on new tonnage for the railway fleet after which the tendering process took place and the ship was ordered. It can be seen that this process represented one huge disadvantage for the nationalised railway fleets who effectively were competing with one hand tied behind their backs.

Immediately following the split from Stena Line, the Swedes also needed to boost their fleet and did so by briefly introducing a 78-metre fast craft *Stena Lynx II* followed in July 1996 by the larger *Stena Lynx III* which crossed from pier to pier in 40 minutes but then took a further ten minutes to berth. Passengers soon realised that there was little to be gained in paying a premium for saving very little time on a vessel with minimal facilities. In addition, Stena brought back the *Stena Cambria* (ex *St Anselm*) from the Irish Sea and introduced the large *Stena Empereur* (ex *Stena Jutlandica*) which, although impressive, was not really suited to the Calais route. She joined the *Stena Fantasia* and *Stena Invicta*, the latter another Scandinavian import which boasted excellent passenger facilities but which only carried 36 x 15-metre freight units.

There was little to fear from this rather eclectic fleet of

Until the final years, SeaFrance refits took place at ARNO's yard in Dunkirk East. Here is the **SeaFrance Manet** high and dry in the company's floating dry dock. (John Hendy)

3 The Calais Years

Top: The **SeaFrance Renoir** *coming astern out of Calais during her final week in service.* (John Hendy)

Above: Renoir's famous painting 'The Boating Party' was reproduced on his SeaFrance namesake's main staircase. (John Hendy)

vessels but when in March 1998 Stena and P&O European Ferries launched their joint venture and P&O took the reins, a far stronger opposition was created. The *Stena Empereur* became the *P&OSL Provence* and the *Stena Fantasia* the *P&OSL Canterbury* and running in tandem with five purpose-built former P&O vessels, efforts were immediately made to improve the on-board standards of the Stena pair and bring them up to P&O levels in terms of on-board experience and, especially, catering.

The joint venture eventually ended in August 2002 after which P&O Ferries operated the service alone.

The year 1998 had been a good one for SeaFrance in which it had improved its results and strengthened its financial position. Turnover rose by 7.4 per cent to FF 1.26 billion and a profit was made for the first time, overturning the previous year's loss of FF 11.8 million. Freight had grown by an impressive 18.1 per cent on the previous year and only foot passenger numbers had dropped. At this early stage in its 16-year history, SeaFrance held 20.4 per cent of the passenger market on the Dover – Calais link and the company had captured some 38.2 per cent of the maritime freight traffic across the short-sea. As much as 75 per cent of the company's traffic was of UK origin. Managing Director Didier Bonnet was able to speak of possible fleet investments of FF 2 billion over the next five years although decisions on the number of new ships required would wait until after 30th June and the ending of Duty-Free concessions. These sales accounted for 40 per cent of SeaFrance's revenue in 1997. M. Bonnet also stated that SeaFrance was attempting to come to terms with its unions concerning strike action which had always been used as a first resort rather than when all the other avenues had been explored. "We need a real change of culture," he said but his wishes were largely ignored.

Following the end of Duty-Free, 1999 was not such a

After her withdrawal in April 2008, the **SeaFrance Manet** *was laid up for several months alongside the former Gare Maritime in Calais. (John Hendy)*

good year for SeaFrance which saw its market share fall. Foot passenger numbers fell dramatically by as much as 56 per cent while freight and coach traffic also suffered. In spite of this, the company still managed to return a profit.

The *SeaFrance Monet* had continued in spasmodic service but her end was sudden when in stormy weather on 29th March 2000, she hit the CA8 buoy when approaching Calais in a NE gale and lost a stabiliser fin. As a result of this incident she took on huge amounts of water and arrived in port in a sinking condition. On her arrival at berth 5 she was blown against the quay by an 80-kph gust and the local fire brigade were called to pump her out. Later three tugs towed her to Dunkirk for lay-up. The company were already without the *SeaFrance Cezanne* which had hit Dover's breakwater a week earlier and so they approached TransEuropa Ferries at Ostend for the charter of their *Larkspur* and also P&O Stena Line for a charter of their *P&OSL Picardy*. Neither company was willing to part with a ship, even in the case of the latter vessel which was laid up and for sale.

SeaFrance decided not to recondition the 'Monet' and immediately offered her for sale. On 18th May she was sold to Naviera Armas SA of Los Palmas for service in the Canary Islands and later towed to Vigo for repairs. Renamed *Volcan de Tacande* she continued to operate until on a voyage to the island of Gomera on 30th January 2005, she hit a rock and lost power after her engine room had flooded resulting in all passengers being evacuated. The ship was declared a total loss and in September 2005 arrived at Aliaga in Turkey for breaking.

During 2000, SeaFrance acquired the 49 per cent which Stena Line held in SPN. The Swedes were happy to sell their share of the company at a loss making $ 8.45 million in order to raise capital for their purchase of the Swedish contribution to Scandlines. The capital raised could not hide a very disappointing 2000 for SeaFrance in which they saw a 25 per cent drop in passenger numbers, a 20 per cent decline in passenger vehicles and a 7 per cent reduction in freight while on-board sales dropped by as much as 50 per

With French yards full to capacity, the excellent **SeaFrance Rodin** *was a product of Aker Finnyards at Rauma in Finland. (FotoFlite)*

THE SeaFrance YEARS

cent in the immediate post Duty-Free era. All this saw a pre-tax profit of FF 50 million in 1999 turn into a loss of FF 50 million in 2000.

NEW TONNAGE AT LAST

In order to secure their flourishing position and to counter the threat posed by the new joint venture, at the end of 1999, SeaFrance were looking to purchase suitable second-hand tonnage and showed interest in Irish Ferries' *Isle of Inishmore*. Unfortunately, the ship in question would not be available for charter or purchase until 2002 and so a new build became the only available choice. However, as all shipyard space in France was full the company had no option but to order their new FF 600 million super ferry from Aker Finnyards at Rauma.

What became the *SeaFrance Rodin* very much represented new territory for the company but Aker Finnyards had been responsible for a number of highly successful and innovative ferries built for the Scandinavian market and so they were undoubtedly in safe hands. Two European yards and one in Asia were short-listed but early in April a letter of intent was sent to Aker which also included the option for a second ship which would be exercised by the end of the year. That this option was not taken up was laid at the feet of instability in the market, continuing trade union problems and a general lack of finances.

Interior design for the new ferry was by AIA Architects in Saint Herblain who had previously worked for both Brittany Ferries and Corsican operators SNCM. AIA had proved that they possessed a good feel for the marine environment and in the 'Rodin' provided all public spaces with both light and dark areas emphasising highlights and giving depth to every area.

Passenger accommodation was spread over two decks which were asymmetrical so that the port side amidships was

3 The Calais Years

*Top: A far brighter colour palette was used in the fitting out of the **SeaFrance Berlioz**. (John Hendy)*

*Above: The **SeaFrance Berlioz**'s a la carte restaurant. (John Hendy)*

given over to ship's offices, galleys etc. On Deck 7 aft, a 400-seater Bar Le Pub was provided with its central U-shaped servery while at the forward end was Le Parisien Bar with its D-shaped dance floor and seats for a further 350 on split levels thereby giving everyone wide views of the sea. Above Le Parisien on Deck 8 was La Brasserie (350 seats) with its semi-circular bar for drinks and snacks in addition to an open plan (no partitioning) waiter service restaurant for 60. Aft of this was a 158-seater lounge and a restaurant for lorry drivers while at the after end was the cafeteria with a further 350 seats. Deck 7 also housed the Tax-Free shopping area which led from the gallery, the attractive but very busy starboard side walkway which linked the passenger accommodation fore and aft and which was joined to Deck 8 via an atrium. This was a unique feature which allowed light to flood into the ship and gave unrivalled views of the surrounding seascape for as many as 1,900 passengers. For the discerning passenger, it was a pity that the vessel did not offer either a Club Class (First Class) lounge or a non-smoking area.

Twin vehicle decks, capable of accommodating 700 cars or 120 x 15-metre lorries were fitted in addition to hoistable car platforms with ramps at either end on the port side of the upper vehicle deck (Deck 5) in order to accommodate a further 95 cars. Particular attention was paid to ventilation in the vehicle deck spaces with 20 changes of air per hour being provided during loading and discharging. On the vehicle decks, there were four lanes to port and three to starboard with an offset central casing. A fast-acting anti-heeling system was provided and operated from either the bridge or the cargo control room while access to the vehicle decks was through clamshell sliding doors. Another 'first' was the covered mooring decks. As the ship's superstructure was carried far forward and the fo'c'sle area was therefore minimal, the enclosed mooring decks not only provided

THE SeaFrance YEARS

cover for those working the machinery but also for the machinery itself.

The ship's bridge was fully enclosed with an efficient cockpit type central control station. Deep windows provided exceptional vision and during docking, the ship's Master was also provided with a deck floor window thereby giving him a direct view of the water level below.

The four Wartsila engines were of the father and son configuration, the larger two each having an output of 11,700kW whilst the son engines each provided 7,800kW. Although capable of 25 knots, there were rarely occasions when this could be used as at both Calais and Dover there is limited berth space and the speed of any particular vessel is effectively regulated by the speed of the vessel ahead and also on the berth to which she has been allocated. There is obviously little point in crossing the Strait in 55 minutes only to have to wait for another 30 minutes to dock. However, if managing to maintain a 25-knot service speed then five round trips each day could be managed which would have allowed the ship to carry some 20km of lorry traffic. On rare occasions, even six round crossings a day were made but even if these fast crossings made economic sense in 2001, it is very doubtful that they would do so today.

The *SeaFrance Rodin* was floated out of the dry-dock in which she was built on 19th May 2001 and, following trials at Dover on 23rd November entered service between Calais and Dover in quite dreadful weather on 29th November during which time she ran late all day. The public relations people referred to her as 'a French masterpiece'. Her introduction increased SeaFrance's freight capacity by 25 per cent.

It was originally intended that the new ship should replace the *SeaFrance Renoir* which retired to Dunkirk for lay-up but buoyed by the success of the service, the ship was retained and continued to play a full and important part in the company's operations. In April 2002 she was unexpectedly revived for a spot charter to Norfolkline, the operators of the Dunkirk – Dover ferry service. With two ships away on refit, the company required a back-up vessel in order to maintain schedules and so an agreement was secured with SeaFrance for an extra daily Calais – Dover working which the 'Renoir' offered. During 2003 the ship was brought back into full-time service but after the arrival of the *SeaFrance Berlioz* in March 2005 her career seemed to be over. In September 2005 the *SeaFrance Renoir* replaced the newer *SeaFrance Manet* on the full-time roster relegating the 'Manet' to freight ship status. The reason for this move lay in the fact that the older ship's accommodation was in a far better condition having had the benefit of an extensive refit during the winter of 1995/96. For a period during 2001, the freight vessel *SeaFrance Nord Pas-de-Calais* was on the sales list but with her passenger certificate for 80, found favour during the summer periods by frequently mopping up traffic left behind by the larger fleet units. She was considered for conversion into a ro-pax mode carrying as many as 400 passengers but this plan came to nothing.

The year 2003 was another disappointing trading year for the company in which freight volumes fell by 15 per cent and passenger numbers by 7 per cent resulting in a loss of £14.7 million for the year. The small *SeaFrance Renoir* continued to operate three times daily but in a freight mode and was on hand to cover the fleet overhaul period during the early part of 2004 although it was intended to withdraw her on the entry into service of the new ship. However, the seamen's union proposed that she should be retained and used to operate a new service to Boulogne but SeaFrance management believed that freight levels would be too low to justify this move. During July 2004, in addition to her freight runs, the ship was also used to operate two extra

3 The Calais Years

daily passenger-carrying crossings before laying up in Dunkirk at the end of August.

The rundown in the Hoverspeed operation (until its eventual closure in 2005) assisted SeaFrance's overall carryings and for the first quarter of the year car numbers were up by 20.6 per cent although foot passenger numbers had continued to dwindle and were down by 39.6 per cent on the same period in 2003.

Such had been the success of the *SeaFrance Rodin* that on 24th June 2004 came the order for a sister ship to be built by Chantiers de l'Atlantique at St Nazaire. The keel of the *SeaFrance Berlioz* was laid on 22nd October, she was floated (launched) on 16th October and she arrived at Calais on 29th March, waiting off Cap Gris Nez for her sister to approach the port from Dover after which the twins entered their home port in line astern. Trials were carried out in Dover the following day although the fog was so thick that very few people were able to witness the occasion. The 'Berlioz' finally entered service on 4th April 2005 with experimental crewing arrangements. The management wanted to operate six ships with the crews of five ships plus an extra 15 personnel. Unfortunately this was not well received by the unions and a series of 24-hour strikes were called. It had been expected that the ship would be delivered during mid-March but a cold winter had interfered with her painting at the yard. Her chosen name came as a result of an internal competition amongst company employees and represented a break from the previous artist names which had been adopted. One of Berlioz's greatest compositions was his epic Symphonie Fantastique of 1830 and needless to say, the ship was immediately hailed as the 'Ferry Fantastique'.

Although structurally identical to the 'Rodin', her interior was far brighter and less restrained with much use of lime greens, oranges and reds while in order to differentiate her

Following the success of the 'Rodin', the **SeaFrance Berlioz** *was a product of Chantiers de l'Atlantique in St Nazaire. (FotoFlite)*

3 The Calais Years

from the 'Rodin', the vertical glazing bars on her bridge windows were painted black. Inevitable problems over crewing once more interrupted the 'Berlioz's' entry into service and although an impressive six-ship timetable was put in place, there was never a time that the SeaFrance vessels were in operation together; a situation that could have done little to improve the company's financial position. In spite of this, during spring 2007 the company were looking to build a third 'Rodin' class ship in addition to a new ro-ro freighter to replace the *SeaFrance Nord Pas-de-Calais*.

The year 2006 was the tenth anniversary of the company's founding and the third passenger ship roster (after the 'Berlioz' and 'Rodin') involved the 'Renoir' for two morning sailings while the 'Cezanne' operated three crossings each afternoon/ evening. The 'NPC' and 'Manet' continued in freight mode. The year was also marked by the award to SeaFrance of the coveted prize for the 'Best Ferry Operator' from group travel organisers across the UK. Encouragingly, SeaFrance achieved growth in all market sectors which were all above the market growth for the route. Thus passenger traffic was up by 11.2 per cent, cars by 7.7 per cent, coaches up 14.8 per cent and freight by 12.7 per cent although the company's detractors would claim that most of this was bought and that any profits generated by this impressive traffic increase were minimal. In 2007 SeaFrance became the official transport partner of the Tour de France which started in London on 7th July. This provided excellent publicity and a bright summer season when many sailings were full.

The SeaFrance management eventually opted for a far more immediate solution to the company's capacity problems. Although the 'Rodin' and 'Berlioz' were state of the art ferries, the 'Cezanne' was starting to show her age while the 'Renoir' and 'Manet' represented a previous generation of ferry construction whose capacity was severely limited. They were now so small that they were no longer economic to operate on the Dover Strait and it was essential to run a service with a balanced fleet. To advertise the service SeaFrance naturally used images of the 'Rodin' and 'Berlioz' but how would passengers react when they found themselves in the 'Manet' which sailed without the benefit of any recent major expenditure or upgrade to her passenger accommodation? It was also unfortunate that the company had transferred many of its best and more reliable staff onto the two new ships and with management/ union relations always in a delicate state there was an underlying groundswell of unhappiness to which unfortunate passengers were all too frequently made aware. Strikes or brief walkouts became commonplace and sadly the service came to lack the reliability and credibility expected of it.

SEAFRANCE MOLIERE – A SHIP TOO FAR?

During the first six months of 2007, SeaFrance announced significant growth in car passenger numbers, which rose by 12.1 per cent, and also enjoyed a buoyant summer period. Throughout this time they carried more traffic than ever before – a rise of 12 per cent – when it was claimed that SeaFrance consistently outperformed the market. In spite of what appeared to be encouraging trading figures, SeaFrance still managed to lose Euro 20.5 million in 2007. However, on the surface all was well and the season allowed SeaFrance to continue with its fleet investment programme. Accordingly, shipyard availability in Europe was sourced for the construction of a new vessel with "significantly increased garage space".

At Calais, changes were afoot with the removal of the older and smaller linkspans at berths 3 and 4 on the west side of the former Gare Maritime. These had latterly exclusively been used by the 'Renoir' and 'Manet' which in future would dock at berth 5 although lay-up periods usually saw them tucked out of the way, alongside at the port's original berths.

On 28th December 2007, SeaFrance announced that they had acquired the ferry *Jean Nicoli* (ex *Superfast X*) on a lease-back charter for Euro 105 million from Mediterranean operators SNCM – a sister French nationalised company. The ship had been introduced on the Rosyth – Zeebrugge service in May 2002 but in August 2006 had been acquired by SNCM for Euro 112 million in order to assist their bid for the Marseilles – Corsica contract. Following this she had almost immediately been offered for resale after which she operated a summer charter to Greek operators ANEK. With accommodation for just 730 passengers and 660 cars, the "significantly increased garage space" was no longer an option.

As the original name of the ship implied, she was indeed super fast and was capable of speeds of up to 28 knots. In order to achieve these speeds, her hull was long and narrow which was not an ideal configuration for carrying large quantities of freight from Calais to Dover. Additionally, the ship was a night ferry with a large number of cabins which required stripping out before commencing her new route. As the majority of passengers were expected to be asleep during their crossings of the North Sea, the ship's public spaces were small and required a degree of opening out prior to taking up service on what, after all, is the most demanding ferry crossing of them all.

A month's strike by SeaFrance offers between February and March 2008 lost the company Euro 5 million and resulted in the usual chaos and inconvenience to P&O Ferries who were again prevented from going about their lawful business by having the Calais berths blocked. SeaFrance announced that they would withdraw the *SeaFrance Renoir* immediately and the 'Manet' in 2009 although this was one of a number of pronouncements that were subsequently modified.

*The **Superfast X** (later **SeaFrance Moliere**) manoeuvring at the Belgian port of Zeebrugge after an overnight sailing from Rosyth. (Mike Louagie)*

SeaFrance took their new ship over in April 2008 and immediately sent her to ARNO at Dunkirk for conversion to day use. A projected Euro 15 million contract became Euro 20 million and delays occurred so that the new ship missed the 2008 peak season.

Passenger cabins were replaced by public spaces and the original passenger certificate was raised to 1,200. Eudes Riblier, the SeaFrance chairman, explained that the name 'Moliere' was seen as an expression of French talent, creativity and way of thinking although one did not have to look very far below the public relations 'hype' to discover the growing discontent which was eventually to kill the company off.

In anticipation of the new ship's arrival, the *SeaFrance Manet* had been withdrawn from service on 29th April operating from Dover to Calais at 21.30 before laying up adjacent to the old Gare Maritime. During her final months in service

The 'Superfast' **SeaFrance Moliere** is seen departing from Calais. (John Hendy)

THE SeaFrance YEARS

she had served in the role of a freight vessel and was just used on a thrice-daily basis. Her withdrawal saw the *SeaFrance Renoir* adopt her schedules until she also finished on 25th July. However, once again she managed to escape withdrawal when it was decided to retain her in a relief role and when in July the Channel Tunnel was closed following its second serious fire, she was quickly brought back into full passenger mode during a period when the ferries operated to capacity across the Dover Strait.

After the inevitable problems over manning the vessel, the *SeaFrance Moliere* was advertised to commence service on 3rd July, 22nd July and then 6th August before finally starting in a freight mode on 19th August. "Teething problems" caused by the Maritime and Coastguard Agency's objections to non-fireproofed carpets and aspects of her sprinkler system saw an advertised entry into full passenger service rearranged for 4th September, 7th September and 23rd September but she eventually commenced full service on 1st October. As there was no Dover 'skywalk' fitted she was unable to carry foot passengers and she was therefore non-standard from the beginning and although undoubtedly an improvement in terms of capacity to the earlier ships, her 110 trucks or 480 cars and 1,200 passengers fell well below the 120 trucks or 700 cars and 1,900 passengers of the 'Rodin' and 'Berlioz'.

Once the *SeaFrance Moliere* had finally entered service, it was the turn of the *SeaFrance Cezanne* to be downgraded to the role of freight ship when her passenger certificate was reduced to just 250. It was also announced that the 'Rodin' and 'Berlioz' would in future be sailing on reduced speeds for between 60 and 80 per cent of their sailings.

The trading season of 2008 was another disaster for SeaFrance with a loss of Euro 22 million. Eudes Riblier took 'gardening leave' and resigned as SeaFrance Chairman in October, ill-health being cited as the reason, and his place was taken by Pierre Fa, the former Inspector General of SNCF.

3 The Calais Years

During mid-December crisis talks were held and SeaFrance brought actions against the ARNO shipyard in Dunkirk and also British sub-contractors that had caused delays to the 'Moliere'. The company's plight was not helped by the entry into service of a rival operation from Boulogne to Dover operated by LD Lines which Robin Wilkins, Managing Director of SeaFrance UK, said "makes life difficult".

With spiralling world fuel prices, an economic recession and over-capacity on the English Channel routes, the vast expense in acquiring and converting the 'Moliere' did nothing to help the serious financial position in which SeaFrance increasingly found themselves; in fact it made matters a whole lot worse. In January 2009 crisis talks were held between SeaFrance and parent company SNCF at which discussions were held to reduce both the size of the workforce and also fleet numbers. The outcome was unacceptable to SNCF who gave the ferry company a further month in which to review their future. A meeting during February decided that 650 jobs would be lost and that only three ships would be operated. With this implemented, SeaFrance announced that they hoped to return to profit by 2010.

The *SeaFrance Cezanne* duly finished service with the 21.35 from Dover on 13th February 2009 after which she went to lay up at Dunkirk joining the 'Manet' but the 'Renoir' was again retained to cover refits and breakdowns. In fact she was reintroduced on the following day when the 'Moliere' was sent to Brest for a month's refit and the 'Berlioz' sailed to the Tyne – the first such occasion following the spat with ARNO at Dunkirk. The last of her generation in service continued in service throughout 2008 and during the early 2009 refit

Swinging off her berth at Dover Eastern Docks in January 2011, the **SeaFrance Rodin** *catches some low winter sunshine. (John Hendy)*

period and then again in May when the new 'Moliere' went off service to Scheldeport with bow-thrust and gearbox problems. However, the 'Moliere's' return to traffic on 26th May finally brought about the inevitable and following her 07.00 sailing from Dover to Calais, the 28-year-old vessel was well and truly 'finished with engines'.

DECLINE AND FALL

In 2005 SeaFrance had made a loss of Euro 27 million but made a net profit of Euro 7.9 million in 2006. In 2007 Euro 20.5 million was lost while in 2008 the company lost Euro 20 million and from October that year continued to lose in the region of Euro 3 million every month.

The initial rescue plans to save SeaFrance were rejected by SNCF on 20th January 2009 as it was stated that they had failed to go far enough. The President of SNCF said that the problems facing the ferry division were caused by the virtual parity of the Euro against the British pound in addition to a failure to adapt the fleet. The freight market had dropped 23 per cent (i.e. by 800,000 fewer trucks) in relation to the same period in 2008.

In the following month, a further restructuring plan was made involving the loss of 650 jobs and the withdrawal of the *SeaFrance Cezanne*, *SeaFrance Renoir* and *SeaFrance Nord Pas-de-Calais*. LD Lines announced that they were interested in taking control of SeaFrance and merging it with their own interests, a suggestion that earned much scorn from both Calais and Paris. Brittany Ferries were also candidates for future input into the company suggesting a 75 per cent stake in a new holding company but wisely decided to retain their power-base in the western Channel.

In July 2009 the redundant *SeaFrance Manet* was sold to Stena Line for service on their Stranraer – Belfast service. She duly arrived at Belfast on 25th September for an extensive refit of her accommodation and reappeared as the *Stena*

Top: The **SeaFrance Nord Pas-de-Calais** *departs from Dover on a morning sailing to Calais in March 2011. (John Hendy)*

Above: An impressive view of the **SeaFrance Berlioz** *arriving off the western pierhead at Calais in September 2009. (John Hendy)*

3 The Calais Years

Arriving at Calais, the **SeaFrance Moliere** *looks every inch a 'greyhound' – an asset that she was unable to use on the 90 minute Dover route. (John Hendy)*

Navigator on 13th November although technical problems were to plague her early service with her new owners. Prior to finishing on 16th November 2011, she had already been sold to Spanish company Eurolineas Maritima SAL (Balearia) for a reported service between Algeciras and Ceuta. After a refit at Santander in February and March 2012 she was renamed *Daniya* and used on the routes from Denia San Antonio to Palma and Barcelona.

Another change occurred on 1st October 2009 when SeaFrance withdrew from the carriage of foot passengers stating that the expense of chartering buses to carry them to and from the ships outweighed the revenue generated from ticket sales.

During December 2009, the efforts to close a deal between SeaFrance and the majority CFDT trade union finally collapsed when 560 employees refused the management offer to save the company and 562 accepted the deal. The union stated that as 60 out of the 63 people in the Paris office had voted in favour, the result of the ballot on the company's future was not representative of the wishes of the seafarers. Grudgingly a deal was eventually signed but then came another strike concerning the management's inflexibility. As there weren't enough ferries to block all the berths at Calais, small boats were now employed to prevent P&O Ferries from docking. SeaFrance was on course to lose Euro 36 million in 2009, this representing about Euro 100,000 a day.

During 2011 some Euro 120 million was injected into SeaFrance in order to keep the company afloat but in early March French financiers reported that they had been unable to find a buyer for the ailing company. In mid-May a commercial tribunal in Paris gave the company a further six

months which was due to end on 27th October.

Meanwhile the sale listed 'Cezanne' and 'Renoir' were finally sold to Belize buyers and renamed *Western Light* and *Eastern Light* for their final voyages for breaking at Alang. The former 'Renoir' left Dunkirk on 21st September and arrived on 31st October while the 'Cezanne' departed on 7th October and arrived on 16th November. Their sale saw Euro 7 million rattle into SeaFrance's empty coffers.

Meanwhile at the end of July, DFDS (operators of the Dunkirk – Dover service) and LD Lines made an impudent Euro 3 offer for SeaFrance although they were not interested in the 'Moliere' which Christophe Santini claimed was not a suitable ship for the route.

At a commercial court hearing in Paris on 16th November 2011, the bids from DFDS/ LD Lines and the CFDT union were rejected and the order was made for the liquidation of SeaFrance. The European Commission had rejected a £176 million rescue plan stating that it was illegal and breached the rules on state aid. SeaFrance would be allowed to continue trading until 28th December but all operations had ceased the day before the hearing and the fleet was laid up. Services were suspended from 04.00 on 15th November. The freighter *SeaFrance Nord Pas-de-Calais* was strikebound at Dover's number 5 berth before plodding her weary way to Dunkirk on 27th. The other three units, with skeleton crews on board, rested at Calais but this time they did not block the linkspans to prevent P&O from berthing. The suspension was initially for 48 hours to safeguard the ships, their passengers and crew but as the company was declared bankrupt, it was unable to pay bunkers, supplies or crew wages.

On 9th January 2012 SeaFrance was officially liquidated and the court invited offers for the company and its assets by 10th May. The liquidator estimated that SeaFrance's accrued debts amounted to Euro 190 million but Euro 240 million was later stated to be the true nature of the losses.

An interesting assessment was made by Robin Wilkins, the Managing Director of SeaFrance UK, during March 2012 when he pointed out that the company's failure to adapt coupled to the recession were the main factors for its demise. He said that everything was too rigid and that it was even impossible to change an item on the menu without senior management's permission. Of the *SeaFrance Moliere*, he said that she was "a big mistake." "When you buy a new vessel it soaks up a lot of funds that you can't claw back straight away. Buying her was a mistake in hindsight because we expected freight volumes to keep getting bigger but in the recession they didn't".

AFTER SEAFRANCE

The meeting on 10th May saw a plan floated for a workers' cooperative to save SeaFrance but their hard line intransigence effectively scuppered any chances they once may have had. Accusations of gangsterism and piracy were made against the local branch of the CDFT union whose head office in Paris had disowned them. There were reports in the French press that union bosses had all but taken control of the SeaFrance management and were operating a mafia-style system of control. Non-union employees complained of violence and intimidation and even the left-wing press made allegations of illegal and unethical practices.

During early May 2012, two bidders made themselves known for the remaining three French ships, the 'Moliere' having sailed to Dunkirk on 22nd February and thence to Tilbury for lay-up. Eurotunnel offered Euro 65 million which was way below the amount that SeaFrance owed. DFDS/LD Lines also made a Euro 50 million bid for the 'Rodin' and 'Berlioz' while Stena Line expressed an interest in the 'Rodin' (for Euro 30 million) but the French Government was anxious to keep the ships under the French flag and retain

3 The Calais Years

Laid up for disposal at Dunkirk East in September 2009, the **SeaFrance Cezanne** *(right) and the* **SeaFrance Renoir** *both ended their days on the beach at Alang in India. (John Hendy)*

500 French jobs. Bids closed on 4th May with Eurotunnel partnering a workers' co-operative in the formation of MyFerryLink.

On 11th June, the bid from Eurotunnel was accepted with them leasing the three ships to MyFerryLink which was essentially a workers' co-operative of former SeaFrance employees.

Services duly restarted without any advance publicity on 20th August when in thick fog, the renamed *Berlioz* arrived at Dover at 06.00 with four cars and a lorry. The *Rodin* duly followed and arrived at 08.15 while the freighter *Nord Pas-de-Calais* eventually entered service on 28th November.

As for the 'Moliere', she was acquired by DFDS and renamed *Dieppe Seaways* to be involved in the rival DFDS/ LD Lines service. Initially it was suggested that she would operate on the company's Dunkirk service but would be placed on the Calais station in the short term to assess her suitability. She took up service on 6th November and was described by the Head of DFDS' Channel Operations as "a great addition to our fleet" – a rather different assessment from the "not suitable" comment made previously by LD's Christophe Santini.

POSTSCRIPT

One of the remarkable things concerning the demise of SeaFrance is that the death of the company was quite so protracted over a relatively long period - rather like one of those operas where towards the end of the first act the heroine is stabbed and takes the rest of the performance to die. One cannot imagine that if SeaFrance was a privately owned company, its death throes would have lasted anywhere nearly as long. That it was a nationalised concern allowed the whole sad saga to be played out across the years until it was finally appreciated that there was really no hope of saving it. Few other companies could have continued to make such hefty losses on a year-by-year basis and hoped to have survived.

As we have seen, the French liked to hold onto their ships until certain units were perhaps past their best and in a position where, to their disadvantage, they were required to compete with newer, larger and more economic tonnage. Thus the *Cote d'Azur* (III) lasted a remarkable 28 years, which is a record for Dover Strait vehicle ferry longevity. Time and time again her owners announced that she was to be withdrawn but, ever the escapologist, she always survived to sail another day. That the train ferry *Saint-Germain* lasted in service for 37 years was an outstanding performance but this was during a time when due to the limitations of Dover's Train Ferry Dock, it was impossible to introduce larger ferries and the economic pressures upon her were not nearly so great. A comparison between the converted sisters *Fantasia* and *Fiesta* of 1990 is of interest in that the French retained their ship (which was later the *SeaFrance Cezanne*) for six years longer than her eventual owners, P&O Ferries, kept the former *Fantasia*.

Towards the end, the six-ship SeaFrance fleet was a mixture of the old and new, the 21st century super-ferries versus the best of the 1980s, the latter unable to cope against opposition vessels more than twice as large. All too frequently ferry companies are judged by their oldest, rather than their newest, ships and exactly the same situation had befallen the nationalised Belgian fleet before its untimely demise in 1997.

The management's acquisition of the *SeaFrance Moliere* was the final nail in the company's coffin from which they could not recover. She was simply a step too far which, given the company circumstances, they just could not afford to take

Top: Having regained her original name with her new owners, the **Nord Pas-de-Calais** *eventually joined the MyFerryLink service in November 2012. (Darren Holdaway)*

Above: The renamed **Berlioz** *commenced the MFL service on 20th August 2012. (FotoFlite)*

3 The Calais Years

and being essentially a night-ship built for high-speed operation, her configuration was quite unsuitable for the type of work that she was expected to perform across the Dover Strait. The 'Rodin' and 'Berlioz' were fine vessels but even they were built for operating at speeds of 25 knots which proved extremely costly both engine and fuel-wise. Such speeds are also nonsensical given the nature of the Calais – Dover link where 22 knots is sufficient to cross in an hour but in reality a 75-90 minute crossing is more suitable in order to allow passengers to take advantage of the extensive facilities and therefore boost on-board sales. Any faster and you just can't get them all through in time.

And then there were the ongoing strikes and problems between the management and unions with which the company was constantly plagued and which appears to be a peculiarly French thing. Whether or not SeaFrance would have survived without the constant agitation from the CFDT union is open to debate but during January 2012, an article in the left-wing newspaper 'Liberation' stated that there were too many French unions competing against each other, acting in their own interests rather than in the interests of their companies and colleagues.

"In the case of SeaFrance, it would seem that there is a complete perversion of what unionism is all about. And it will not save SeaFrance".

The MyFerryLink service was started without any prior advertising as a result of which, the ships initially sailed almost empty. Here the **Rodin** arrives at Dover in the first month. (John Hendy)

Fleet List

Name	Built / In service / Withdrawn	Builder	Gross tons / Passengers / Vehicles	Notes

Dieppe - Newhaven

Name	Built / In service / Withdrawn	Builder	Gross tons / Passengers / Vehicles	Notes
Bordeaux	1912 / 1912 / 1951	Ateliers et Chantiers de la Loire, St Nazaire	774 / cargo vessel	1951: replaced by the Brest
Worthing (British flag)	1928 / 1928 / 1954	Wm Denny & Bros, Dumbarton	2,288 / 1,300	1955: sold to John S Latsis (Greece), renamed Phryne. Scrapped 1964
Londres (British flag from 1955)	1941 / 1947 / 1963	Forges & Chantiers de la Mediterranee, Le Havre	2,434 / 1,450	Sold to Typaldos Bros (Greece), renamed Sophoklis Venizelos. Scrapped 1966
Nantes	1946 / 1946 / 1965	Chantiers et Ateliers de St Nazaire, Rouen	999 / cargo vessel / 60	1966: sold Metaxas & Co (Greece) renamed Lassi II. Resold 1967 to Yassemis of Jeddah (Saudi Arabia) renamed Eny. 3.1969: stranded on Na'man Island in Red Sea.
Arromanches	1947 / 1947 / 1964	Forges & Chantiers de la Mediterranee, Le Havre	2,600 / 1,450	Sold to Nomikos (Greece), renamed Leto. Scrapped 1973
Rennes	1948 / 1948 / 1965	Chantiers et Ateliers de St Nazaire, Rouen	1,053 / cargo vessel / 60	1966: sold Metaxas & Co (Greece) renamed Lassi III. 1968: renamed Diana. Scrapped 1974.
Brighton (British flag)	1950 / 1950 / 1966	Wm Denny & Bros, Dumbarton	2,875 / 1,450	Sold to Jersey Lines, renamed La Duchesse de Bretagne. Scrapped 1970.
Brest	1951 / 1951 / 1966	Chantiers et Ateliers de St Nazaire, Rouen	1,037 / cargo vessel / 60	1966: closed cargo service thereafter working at Folkestone and Weymouth. 1967: sold Metaxas & Co (Greece) renamed Lassi IV. 1968: resold to Tannous of Beirut (Lebanon) and renamed Samir. 1970: sold to Pan Arabian Trading, renamed Brigitte S. 1972: renamed Huda. 1972: sold to Wafic Begdache, renamed Mahdi.
Lisieux	1953 / 1953 / 1965	Forges & Chantiers de la Mediterranee, Le Havre	2,946 / 1,450	Sold to Nomikos (Greece), renamed Apollon. 1976: resold to Agapitos Bros (Greece) Scrapped 1982.
Falaise (British flag)	1947 / 1964 / 1973	Wm Denny & Bros, Dumbarton	2,416 / 700 / 100	1964: converted to car ferry. 1973: transferred to Weymouth. Scrapped 1974
Villandry	1965 / 1965 / 1982	Dubigeon-Normandie, Nantes	3,444 / 1,200 / 140	1976: converted to drive-through at Le Havre. 1982: transferred to Calais. 1984: sold to Agapitos Bros (Greece) renamed Olympia.. 1986: resold to Strintzis Lines (Greece). Scrapped 1998.
Valencay	1965 / 1965 / 1984	Chantiers de Atlantique, St Nazaire	3,430 / 1,200 / 140	1977: converted to drive-through at Le Havre. 1984: sold Strintzis Lines (Greece) renamed Eptanisos, 2000: resold to Ventouris Lines (Greece), renamed Pollux. Scrapped 2003.
Capitaine Le Goff	1972 / 1972 / 1978	Hatio Verksted A/S, Ulsteinvik (Norway)	499 / 12 / 25 lorries + 25 cars	Roll on – roll off freighter, built as Admiral Carrier I. 1982: sold to Baaboud & Co (Saudi Arabia) renamed Al Zaher II. Scrapped 2008.

THE SeaFrance YEARS

Name	Built / In service / Withdrawn	Builder	Gross tons / Passengers / Vehicles	Notes
Senlac (British flag until 1985)	1973 / 1973 / 1987	Brest Naval Dockyard	5,590 / 1,200 / 256 cars or 38 lorries /80 cars	1985: sold to SNCF. 1987: sold to Ventouris Sea Lines (Greece) renamed Apollo Express then Apollo Express 1 in 1993. 1996: resold to Agapitos Express Ltd, renamed Express Apollon. 1999: resold to Minoan Dolphins. 2006: resold and renamed Apollon in 2007. Scrapped 2010.
Cornouailles	1977 / 1984 / 1986	Tronheims Mek Verksted, Norway	3,383 / 550 / 205	On charter from Brittany Ferries who sold her to British Channel Island Ferries in 1988 - renamed Havelet. 2000: sold to Montenegro Lines, renamed Sveti Stefan. Scrapped 2013.
Versailles/ SeaFrance Monet	1974 / 1986 / 2000	Brodogradiliste Jozo Lozovina Mosor, Togir, Yugoslavia	6,333 / 1,800 / 425	Built as Stena Nordica for Stena Line (Sweden). 1974: renamed Stena Danica, 1981: renamed Srena Nordica. 1983: chartered to RMT (Ostend) and renamed Stena Nautica in 1984, 1986: chartered to SNCF – renamed Versailles, 1988: sold to SNCF. 1992: chartered to Sealink Stena Line, renamed Stena Londoner. 1996: to SeaFrance as SeaFrance Monet. 2000: sold to Naviera Armas renamed Volcan de Tacande. Scrapped 2005.

Dunkirk - Dover train ferry

Name	Built / In service / Withdrawn	Builder	Gross tons / Passengers / Vehicles	Notes
Twickenham Ferry	1934 / 1936 / 1974	Swan, Hunter & Wigham Richardson, Wallsend-on-Tyne	2,839 / 500 / 12 sleeping cars or 40 goods wagons, 25 cars	1936: transferred to Southern Railway's French subsidiary co – ALA. Scrapped 1974
Saint-Germain	1951 / 1951 / 1988	Helsingor Shipyard, Denmark	3,094 / 850 / 12 sleeping cars or 40 goods wagons, 25 cars or 135 cars	Scrapped 1988
Saint Eloi/ Channel Entente	1972 / 1975 / 1988	Cantieri Navali di Petra Ligure, Genoa, Italy	4,649 / 1,000 / 12 sleeping cars or 40 wagons, 25/160 cars	Owned by ALA. 1988 summer – Calais – Dover W. Docks on charter to SNCF thence to Irish Sea. 1989: renamed Channel Entente. 1990: sold Isle of Man SP Co – renamed King Orry. Sold 1998 to Moby Lines (Italy), renamed Moby Love then Moby Love 2. 2002 renamed Moby Love.
Transcontainer 1	1969 / 1969 / 1986	CNIM, La Seyne	2,760 / 36	Built for Dunkirk–Harwich. 1974: to Dover route. 1975: Dunkirk West – 36 wagons. Felixstowe. 1985: Dieppe – Portsmouth, 1986: Dunkirk West – Dover.1986: sold to Pireo Cia, Nav. SA (Greece). 1991: resold Panamanian owners renamed Nour 1 for service to Jordan. Resold in 1995 (renamed Niobe 1) and again in 1995 to Rainbow Lines. Scrapped 2000
Nord Pas-de-Calais	1987 / 1987	Chantiers du Nord et de la Mediterranee, Dunkirk	13,727 / 80 / 45 lorries + 600 m of rail freight	Train ferry service between 1988-1995 thence freight on Calais Calais – Dover. 1996: renamed with SeaFrance prefix. 2012: to MyFerryLink - original name restored

Fleet List

Name	Built / In service / Withdrawn	Builder	Gross tons / Passengers / Vehicles	Notes
Calais – Dover				
Cote d'Azur	1950 / 1950 / 1972	F & C de la Mediterranee, Le Havre	3,998 / 1,336	Used on Folkestone services. Sold to SA Monegasque d'Armement et de Navigation, renamed Marie F. Scrapped 1974
Compiegne	1958 / 1958 / 1981	Chantiers Reunis Loire-Normandie, Rouen	3,467 / 1,000 / 164	Sold Strintzis Lines (Greece) renamed Ionian Glory. 1989: sold Vergina Lines (Cyprus) and renamed Queen Vergina. 1990: sold Liano Shipping Co (Malta) renamed Freedom 1. 1994: sold Raneem Maritime Transport (Saudi Arabia) renamed Katerina. 1995: sold Waad Shipping Co (Honduras) renamed Al Amirah – laid up Alexandria, later renamed Al Ameerah. 2013 – scrapped?
Chantilly	1966 / 1966 / 1984	Dubigeon-Normandie, Nantes	3,255 / 1,350 / 200	1976: converted to drive through. Dieppe – Newhaven 1986-87. 1987: sold Agapitos Bros (Greece) renamed Olympia. 1990: sold Bahamian owners for Moroccan service. 1993: resold to Liberian co for Polish service – renamed Baltavia. 1996: sold to Al Salaam Maritime (Egypt) – renamed El Salaam 93. Scrapped 2003
Chartres	1973 / 1973 / 1993	Dubigeon-Normandie, Nantes	4,590 / 1,400 / 240 cars or 40 freight vehicles	Between 1982-89 on the Dieppe – Newhaven link. 1993: sold Agapitos Bros (Greece) renamed Express Santorini. 1999: sold Minoan Flying Dolphins. Since 2007: chartered to Atlanticoline for summer service in Azores
Cote d'Azur / SeaFrance Renoir	1981 / 1981 / 2009	Ateliers et Chantiers du Havre, Le Havre	8,862 / 1,600 / 330 cars or 43 lorries	Renamed in 1996. Scrapped 2011
Champs Elysees / SeaFrance Manet	1984 / 1984 / 2008	Dubigeon-Normandie, Nantes	9,069 / 1,800 / 330 cars / 43 lorries	1990: switched to Dieppe – Newhaven. 1992: chartered to Sealink Stena Line renamed Stena Parisien. 1997: renamed SeaFrance Manet for service at Calais. Withdrawn 2008. Sold to Stena Line - 2009-11 renamed Stena Navigator. 2012: sold to Balearia (Spain) and renamed Daniya
Fiesta / SeaFrance Cezanne	1980 / 1990 / 2009	Kockums Varv, Malmo (Sweden)	25,122 / 1,800 / 640 cars / 80 lorries	Operated as a deep-sea ro-ro vessel named Ariadne (1980), Soca (1980), Trapezitza (1981). 1988: sold Sealink UK Ltd and renamed Fantasia. 1989: renamed Channel Seaway. 1989-90 rebuilt as passenger ferry and renamed Fiesta. 1996: renamed SeaFrance Cezanne. Withdrawn 2009, scrapped 2011.
SeaFrance Rodin	2001 / 2001 / 2011	Aker Finnyards, Rauma (Finland)	33,796 / 1,900 / 700 cars/120 lorries	Withdrawn 2011. MyFerryLink 2012 renamed Rodin
SeaFrance Berlioz	2004 / 2004 / 2011	Chantiers Atlantique, St Nazaire	33,796 / 1,900 / 700 cars/120 lorries	Withdrawn 2011. MyFeryLink 2012, renamed Berlioz
SeaFrance Moliere	2002 / 2008 / 2011	Deutsche Werft AG, Kiel (Germany)	30,285 / 1,200 / 410 cars / 110 lorries	Built as Superfast X for Superfast Ferries (Greece). 2006: sold to SNCM (Corsica) and renamed Jean Nicoli. 2007: acquired by SeaFrance and renamed SeaFrance Moliere. Withdrawn 2011. 2012: renamed Moliere – later chartered to DFDS Seaways and renamed Dieppe Seaways